The Opportunity Analysis Canvas
for Student Entrepreneurs

Third Edition

James V. Green

Publication Data

Green, James V.

The opportunity analysis canvas for student entrepreneurs / James V. Green

Third edition

1. Entrepreneur. 2. Innovation.

ISBN: 978-1090934697

For Jamesia, Alexandra, and Vivian.

Thank you for giving me the opportunity every day to be a husband and dad.

About the Author

An award-winning educator and entrepreneur, Dr. James V. Green leads the education activities of the Maryland Technology Enterprise Institute (Mtech) at the University of Maryland. As its Director of Entrepreneurship Education, he leads the undergraduate and graduate courses and programs in entrepreneurship, innovation, and technology commercialization. He has created and led a host of innovative programs and activities that serve over 800,000 entrepreneurs and innovators from over 175 countries. With more than 20 publications to his credit, he is a thought leader in entrepreneurship education.

In 2011, he won the 3E Learning Innovative Entrepreneurship Education Competition presented at the United States Association for Small Business and Entrepreneurship (USASBE). In 2013, he launched the University of Maryland's first MOOC with Coursera's "Developing Innovative Ideas for New Companies".

Prior to joining the University of Maryland, Dr. Green held founder, executive, and operational roles with multiple startups, including WaveCrest Laboratories (an innovator in next-generation electric and hybrid-electric propulsion and drive systems, acquired by Magna International, NYSE: MGA), Cyveillance (a software startup and world leader in cyber intelligence and intelligence-led security, acquired by QinetiQ, LSE: QQ.L), and NetMentors.Org (the first national online career development eMentoring community).

Dr. Green earned a Doctor of Management and an MS in Technology Management from the University of Maryland Global Campus, an MBA from the University of Michigan, and a BS in Industrial Engineering from the Georgia Institute of Technology.

Access Code for the Online Simulation

For students enrolled in a course that's adopted the online simulation for The Opportunity Analysis Canvas, please contact your faculty for instructions on how to register with your unique access code.

Contents

Chapter 1. Introduction

There is nothing more powerful than an idea whose time has come.

Victor Hugo

Poet, novelist, and dramatist

30,188.

At the time of this writing, this is the number of results when searching for business plan books on Amazon.com. As we need the business idea before writing the business plan, aspiring entrepreneurs require insight and direction on how to identify and analyze entrepreneurial ideas. This book stands alone in its focus on integrating entrepreneurial thinking, seeing, and acting upon entrepreneurial opportunities. It will help you find that idea from which to build a new venture.

What is an opportunity?

In this context, the term *opportunity* refers to the potential to create a new venture. This can be a for-profit company, a non-profit company, a venture within an established company or organization, or any related venture that creates value for the customers and the owners of the venture.

Why are there millions of missed opportunities?

In retrospect, we all recognize good opportunities. It's easy to see the successes of others, and believe that we could have achieved similar success had we acted on our own past ideas. Our decisions, however, are of most value in the present, and not in hindsight.

Each year, over one million students enroll in entrepreneurship courses worldwide. Estimates suggest that less than 2% of these students actually launch a business. Why are so few students launching businesses? While many students are interested in solely learning skills for future use, a significant number do desire to launch a new venture in the near term. This mismatch of entrepreneurial ambitions versus actually launching ventures exists for students of all ages.

What's missing?

There is the need for something new, something different, that helps us identify and analyze entrepreneurial opportunities. For aspiring entrepreneurs, new tools are necessary to develop the ideas that can lead to effective business planning and successful ventures.

Is the business model approach the key?

The *business model* is the precursor to the *business plan*. The emergence of business model courses and competitions in universities, in lieu of prematurely writing business plans, is a step in the right direction. The focus of these new business model courses and activities is to engage aspiring entrepreneurs in customer discovery early. An emphasis is placed on testing the major hypotheses of the business model before investing significant effort and capital into creating the business plan or the business itself.

While this is a viable approach, and a valuable lesson in entrepreneurship education, business models can only begin to take shape after a new venture idea is formulated. Customer discovery requires having a product or service concept to test.

What is the Opportunity Analysis Canvas?

The Opportunity Analysis Canvas is based on my experiences of teaching over 800,000 students and advising hundreds of companies including multiple *Inc. 500* award winners.

This canvas began over 10 years ago with my doctoral dissertation titled "Educating entrepreneurship students about opportunity discovery: A psychosocial development model for enhanced decision-making." While this dissertation title may sound complicated, the basic idea is that before drafting business models and writing business plans, aspiring entrepreneurs need to see and think about problems and solutions differently than others.

As I explored this topic of entrepreneurial opportunity analysis, I recognized a pattern that could be identified. With that identification and understanding, I saw that it is a process that could be taught.

Before beginning this book, over many years at the University of Maryland, I tested various ideas and approaches of teaching. These activities engaged thousands of my students in readings, assignments, projects, and mentoring that led to dramatic improvement in their entrepreneurial opportunity identification and analysis skills.

The outcome of this opportunity analysis journey, and the proven success of its teaching, is this book. It is my hope that by understanding the principles and patterns of the Opportunity Analysis Canvas you will become more effective in identifying and analyzing entrepreneurial opportunities, and realizing your personal and professional goals.

The Opportunity Analysis Canvas is a new tool for identifying and analyzing entrepreneurial ideas. Structured as a nine-step experience, the canvas is segmented into: thinking entrepreneurially with an *entrepreneurial mindset, entrepreneurial motivation,* and *entrepreneurial behavior;* seeing entrepreneurially with *industry condition, industry status, macroeconomic change,* and *competition;* and acting entrepreneurially with *value innovation* and *opportunity identification.*

The Opportunity Analysis Canvas

Without the idea for the product or service, neither business model nor customer discovery can begin. It is this first step of defining the idea that the Opportunity Analysis Canvas aims to fulfill.

How can you best use this book?

This book's structure directly aligns with the Opportunity Analysis Canvas, as each of the nine steps is addressed in a dedicated chapter. The focus of each chapter is to first introduce you to the topic. This provides a background on the subject and describes its relationship to entrepreneurship. Tools including research databases and reference materials are highlighted. Tips and techniques are then presented for how to develop your skills and knowledge. A featured entrepreneur is then profiled. Lastly, challenge questions are posed for you to develop your opportunity analysis abilities.

These nine steps are explored in three parts.

Steps 1 – 3: Thinking entrepreneurially. Thinking in this context is influenced by individual mindsets, motivations, and behaviors. Part I addresses these first three steps of the Opportunity Analysis Canvas. This sets the stage for the subsequent chapters on seeing entrepreneurially.

Steps 4 – 7: Seeing entrepreneurially. Part II examines seeing entrepreneurially, which requires that you have a "big picture" perspective. This means that you recognize and understand the economic forces impacting your ideas as well as industry and competitive factors that exist now and in the future. With dedicated chapters on industry condition, industry status, macroeconomic change, and competition, each of these steps is explored in detail.

Steps 8 – 9: Acting entrepreneurially. As you develop your abilities to think and see entrepreneurially, you are better prepared to act. With attention to value innovation and opportunity identification, your entrepreneurial ideas can be transformed into action.

Chapter 2. What are entrepreneurial opportunities?

Don't start a company unless it's an obsession and something you love.
If you have an exit strategy, it's not an obsession.

Mark Cuban

American entrepreneur, investor, and owner
of the NBA's Dallas Mavericks and AXS TV

To explore the roles of entrepreneurial thinking and opportunity identification, an introduction to *entrepreneurial opportunities* is in order.

As we examine entrepreneurial opportunities, we're going to spend this chapter discussing the foundational elements of entrepreneurship. We'll also explore modern interpretations of the term entrepreneurial opportunities and discuss emerging opportunities.

Casson defines entrepreneurial opportunities as "those situations in which new goods, services, raw materials, and organizing methods can be introduced and sold at greater than their cost of production." [1]

---

[1] Casson, M. (1982). The Entrepreneur. Totowa, NJ, US: Barnes and Noble Books.

Drucker classifies entrepreneurial opportunities into three categories: "(1) the creation of new information, as occurs in the invention of new technologies; (2) the exploitations of market inefficiencies that result from information asymmetry, as occurs across time and geography; and (3) the reaction to shifts in the relative costs and benefits of alternative uses for resources, as occurs with political, regulatory, or demographic changes." [2]

By all definitions, entrepreneurial opportunities differ from the larger set of general business opportunities. Entrepreneurial opportunities require the discovery of new relationships and interactions in the marketplace that are uncertain and dynamic.[3,4]

Differences of opinion by individuals may highlight entrepreneurial opportunities, with some seeing opportunities while others view the same situation with doubt or disinterest.[5,6] Therefore, understanding decision-making in the context of entrepreneurial thinking is central to joining this population that sees opportunities.

[2] Drucker, P.F. (1985). Innovation and Entrepreneurship. New York: Harper & Row.

[3] Baumol, W. (1993). "Formal entrepreneurship theory in economics: Existence and bounds," Journal of Business Venturing, Vol. 8 No. 3: pp. 197-210.

[4] Kirzner, I. (1997). "Entrepreneurial discovery and the competitive market process: An Austrian approach," Journal of Economic Literature, Vol. 35: 60-85.

[5] Hayek, F.A. (1945). "The use of knowledge in society," American Economic Review, Vol. 35: 519–530.

[6] Kirzner, I. (1973). Competition and Entrepreneurship. Chicago: University of Chicago Press.

How have entrepreneurs evolved over history?

When we look at the history of opportunity and how humans have created value over time, and what has been at the forefront of being able to do that, at first it was the hunter, the grower, and the warriors. It then became the craftsmen and the explorers, and the merchants and the mechanizers. It went on to the industrialists. More recently, it's the corporate path, the corporate executive. Today, investment banking and private equity are popular career ambitions.

What is the next phase as we think about where great value will be derived? Where are those individuals with the highest need for achievement going to be attracted?

It's the startup companies. It's those who can make useful things faster than corporations. It's those willing to take larger risks for larger rewards. By being more innovative and creating more value in the marketplace, startups will lead the future.

In addition to full-time entrepreneurs, we see entrepreneurial activities via independent contractors and side-preneurs.

Independent contractors are gaining a lot of momentum in the U.S. and globally. Outsourcing, traditionally limited to manufacturing and call centers, is taking hold in software development and research and development (R&D). There are a variety of different pieces of the organization that are being outsourced. In many cases, it's small, entrepreneurial firms that are playing a role in providing that outsourcing.

Side-preneurs have a day job, but they also work nights, or weekends, or on their days off on independent projects for hire. These projects are typically in their field of expertise. They may be employed as a graphic designer by day with a company, but they're also going to do graphic design work at night for other individuals outside of their company.

We're also seeing entrepreneurship growing via new online communities. New marketplaces are emerging whereby for reasonable affordability, entrepreneurs and small businesses, and even large businesses, can contract out jobs to freelancers online to deliver that work. Cumulative transactions for these online communities are in excess of a billion dollars. Leading companies in this category include Upwork, Freelancer, 99 designs, and dozens of others. I've personally used a number of these services for my own projects.

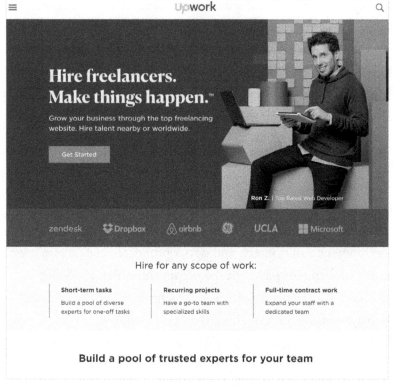

Figure 1. Upwork Website

When we look at the number of freelancers who are out there, the number of people who are doing graphic design, the number of people who are writing web copy, the number of people who are doing computer programming assignments and tasks, the total number exceeds 10 million. When you look at the number of jobs that have been posted, we see tremendous numbers there—millions and millions of jobs posted.

The economics work for the freelancer. If you pay a $300 fee to Upwork—to have a logo designed, for example—10% of that will stay with Upwork, and that's essentially their management fee. The remaining 90% goes to the individual who's actually designing that logo. This often exceeds their compensation for completing a similar project as an employee of a large company.

Futurists who are thinking about the businesses of the future forecast that many more of us will become entrepreneurs. They see employee healthcare and financial benefits, pension plans and retirement packages, all disappearing in the future for most employees of most companies. Everybody's going to be a free agent, and everybody's going to be an entrepreneur. You're going to broker your skills and negotiate your own contracts for everything. Now it may not reach 100% of companies, but it certainly is an interesting future to think about, and it's an interesting concept to be aware of on the path to becoming an entrepreneur.

Entrepreneurship continues to evolve over time, as do the opportunities that entrepreneurs pursue.

How have entrepreneurial opportunities changed over time?

Software and hardware entrepreneurs have monopolized discussions of startups in recent decades. While Bill Gates, Steve Jobs, Elon Musk, and our modern celebrity entrepreneurs are creating tremendous products and new markets, they're neither the first nor the wealthiest entrepreneurs in history.

In the Gilded Age in the U.S. during the late 1800s, new factories, oil production, shipping, lumber, and railroads generated tremendous sums of wealth for entrepreneurs. A top 10 list of entrepreneurs in their day would read John D. Rockefeller, Jay Gould, Henry Clay Frick, Andrew W. Mellon, Andrew Carnegie, Henry Flagler, Henry H. Rogers, J. P. Morgan, Leland Stanford, and Cornelius Vanderbilt.

In the century prior, mechanization during the Industrial Age created another generation of entrepreneurs who identified and acted on opportunities. Benjamin Franklin and James Watt were of this class.

While the term *entrepreneur* is popular today, the practice of entrepreneurship has been ever-present in society.

Today, we see the influence of entrepreneurs on a global scale. Unprecedented globalization is taking place with new access to financial capital, partners, and customers. One way to quantify that is through rising GDP among nations. Heightened wealth and a larger middle class globally can buy items that were once unaffordable. This new middle class can participate in markets with access to new products and services. Consider the opportunity that this presents to aspiring entrepreneurs.

We also see that the adoption rate of new products and new technologies is rapidly rising. From the time that automobiles, washing machines, and telephones were invented, it took over 20 years for them to reach an 80% adoption rate in the market. Modern technologies – cell phones, the Internet, and personal computers – have in a very short time span reached 60%, 80%, even 90% market penetration in less than 10 years. This rate of adoption of new technologies is unprecedented.

Virtual teams and a global network of collaborators are now easier to establish than ever. I can find co-founders and advisors with CoFoundersLab. LegalZoom, in the U.S., can assist with my corporate formation and provisional patents. I can crowdfund my idea while reaching customers globally via KickStarter, and secure equity funding via Crowdcube in London. I'll use Upwork to hire my development team in the Middle East. With Fiverr I can spend $10 on a logo designed in South America.

The globalization of entrepreneurship also brings unparalleled competition. These terrific online networks and collaborators are available to your competitors as well. Those of us with entrepreneurial ideas need to execute on them reasonably soon. A good idea now will be someone else's business later if you don't execute.

We will examine how to be better, faster decision makers. We will discuss how to bring our ideas to market quickly, and how to leverage the changes taking place with new technologies and new products, to capitalize on the globalization of entrepreneurship.

What is Amazon.com's approach to entrepreneurial opportunities?

The history of Amazon is an example of how to identify and act on entrepreneurial opportunities. In 1994, Amazon set out to sell books on the Internet at an affordable price and with a selection of titles as vast as the Amazon rainforest. A decade later, Amazon was a leader in printed books and CD-based music. It soon became a leader in DVD sales as well.

Today, the majority of their sales are from media and digital goods, not their historic strongholds of physical products. Amazon is not waiting. They did not wait to see what would happen with eBook adoption in the marketplace. They did not wait long to see what happened with online music. They're not waiting to see what happens with artificial intelligence, cloud computing, and machine learning. They're leading the charge.

We will explore what they've done to enter new markets, be leaders in these spaces, and not be comfortable as the successful incumbent. Amazon is an interesting company to examine, and a company that we will continue to explore in this book.

What is our approach to studying entrepreneurial opportunities?

Entrepreneurial opportunities differ from the general set of business opportunities. There are new relationships that are uncertain and dynamic. There are always new players involved. There is a race to bring new products and technologies to market.

I aim to help you understand that opportunity identification is a critical first step to success as an entrepreneur. Together, we will improve your ability to see entrepreneurial opportunities and make entrepreneurial decisions. You will be better prepared to make decisions that have significant consequences quickly and comfortably. You can more confidently take the necessary steps to capitalize on your entrepreneurial ideas.

When we discuss entrepreneurial opportunities, this is a term that is well entrenched in universities and research centers, and widely studied in recent decades. I will bring information to you from the academic arena as well as from the practical arena based on my experience as a founder, executive, adviser, and investor with startup companies. Through this book, you can validate or enhance opportunities that you are already considering, and identify new entrepreneurial opportunities.

Decision making is the foundation for entrepreneurial success. While we could skip this topic of decision making, and dive into how you create business models or marketing plans, we recognize the value of decision making and the importance of the *entrepreneur* in *entrepreneur*ship. It all starts with the entrepreneur. For us, the next step is a discussion on strategic decision making.

Chapter 3. What is strategic decision making?

When you're first thinking through an idea, it's important not to get bogged down in complexity. Thinking simply and clearly is hard to do.

Richard Branson

Founder of Virgin Group (400+ companies including Virgin America, Virgin Atlantic Airways, Virgin Cola, Virgin Galactic, Virgin Media, Virgin Mobile, Virgin Money, and Virgin Records)

As we examine decision making, and specifically strategic decision making, we'll explore the term in an entrepreneurial context. We'll continue our discussion of Amazon, and the elements that motivated them to select the product categories that they began with. We'll also introduce the concept of cognition, and connect cognition to the entrepreneurial process.

Decisions typically share a similar path. We recognize a problem. We generate alternatives. We evaluate those alternatives. Then, we select the alternative that best satisfies our evaluation criteria. This is true for many different types of decisions, including major personal decisions such as buying a home or an automobile. Strategic professional decisions include career changes. Entrepreneurial decisions include what to launch, if to launch, and how to launch our venture.

In the beginning of the venture, nearly all decisions are strategic: when you're evaluating the idea, when you're thinking about the concept, when you're developing the prototype, when you're testing that with customers, and when you're considering if you need to raise funding.

Before bringing your product to market, strategic decisions include:

- Who should be your co-founders?
- What should you focus on in your marketing plan?
- How do you build the product?
- Where do you build it?
- What do you spend on building it?

What was Amazon.com's first strategic decision?

As an example of entrepreneurial strategic decision making, consider the ideal product to sell online in 1994. The answer would be quite different than what it would be today.

Today, we have decades of experience and research on online sales. We have millions of articles, reports, magazines, case studies, and books on online sales. There are even movies based on entrepreneurial success stories for online businesses, to include *The Social Network* in 2010, adapted from Ben Mezrich's 2009 book *The Accidental Billionaires: The Founding of Facebook*.

In 1994, at the birth of online retailing, research materials were very scarce. There were general business principles that made sense, such as thinking strategically about what could I sell online, and that online retailing presented possible advantages to bricks and mortar retailing. There was a question of convenience. Was it something that customers needed immediately? Was shipping affordable for certain product types? Could customers envision the product without seeing it in person?

There are other factors in the mid-1990s that made the Internet different than it is now. Security is one. If I've never bought anything online, am I willing to enter my credit card information online? Am I willing to buy things from companies I've never heard of? And what's the consequence of that? As a consumer, am I willing to risk $10? $100? When we look at these considerations, we ask, what's the ideal product to sell online?

For Amazon, it was books first and music second. Specifically, printed books and CDs made sense. We'll talk about why they made sense.

Welcome to Amazon.com Books!

One million titles, consistently low prices.

(If you explore just one thing, make it our personal notification service. We think it's very cool!)

SPOTLIGHT! -- AUGUST 16TH
These are the books we love, offered at Amazon.com low prices. The spotlight moves **EVERY** day so please come often.

ONE MILLION TITLES
Search Amazon.com's million title catalog by author, subject, title, keyword, and more... Or take a look at the books we recommend in over 20 categories... Check out our customer reviews and the award winners from the Hugo and Nebula to the Pulitzer and Nobel... and bestsellers are 30% off the publishers list...

EYES & EDITORS, A PERSONAL NOTIFICATION SERVICE
Like to know when that book you want comes out in paperback or when your favorite author releases a new title? Eyes, our tireless, automated search agent, will send you mail. Meanwhile, our human editors are busy previewing galleys and reading advance reviews. They can let you know when especially wonderful works are published in particular genres or subject areas. Come in, meet Eyes, and have it all explained.

YOUR ACCOUNT
Check the status of your orders or change the email address and password you have on file with us. Please note that you **do not** need an account to use the store. The first time you place an order, you will be given the opportunity to create an account.

Figure 2. Amazon.com's First Website (1995)

One element was the competition in books and music retailing, which was characterized by a large, fragmented market. There were the mall retailers like Waldenbooks, B. Dalton, Crown Books, Sam Goody, Musicland, Suncoast and others in the U.S. But with no major players, competition was widely distributed.

Books and music were also attractive online products to retail because you knew exactly what you were getting when you ordered a certain title online. We did not need to try it on or taste it. It wasn't a consumer electronic device that you wanted to see working in the store, or see the quality of the picture before we bought a television. We knew that if a book was from a certain author and a certain title, or that a CD was of a certain album from a certain artist, it would be exactly what we expected.

Searching was very easy to do as well. Books and music did not come in multiple sizes, multiple widths, and multiple colors. As consumers, we could easily search and find what we were looking with books and music.

Books and music brought large market opportunities for Amazon. What this means is that millions of Americans read books, and many more listened to music.

There was an element of product branding that Amazon was able to leverage and integrate. Even though people did not know what Amazon was then, they knew the books that they loved and the music they loved. They knew John Grisham, Tom Clancey, Stephen King, Madonna, and Michael Jackson.

By bypassing the bricks-and-mortar expenses, there was a cost advantage. Amazon saved retail space cost and associated labor cost. They could share those savings with customers.

Shipping costs for books and music was inexpensive.

Books and music made a lot of sense as an online purchase in the mid-1990s.

Even with these advantages, if you've studied Amazon, you know that it took until 2003 to achieve profitability. They built tremendous market share and an incredible brand along the way.

But they didn't stop there.

The books and the music of the 1990s was where they started. They've done infinitely more things since then, particularly in the digital space, as we'll discuss. Remember that it started with a very strategic decision of doing one simple thing well, selling books online.

What are the characteristics of strategic decisions?

When we discuss strategic decisions, there are four fundamental characteristics to consider. These are:

- Complexity - What really makes a decision strategic is that it's complex. There are lots of facts, variables, and alternative choices. There's not an easy answer.

- Uncertainty - We don't know the eventual outcome. We can anticipate and plan and forecast, but we're not sure. So, there is an element of the unknown.

- Rationality - There are limits of rationality to consider. What are our goals? What are our objectives?

- Control - We can control, or at least influence, some factors, albeit not all.

In this way, when we think about strategic decisions, these four characteristics come into play.

Why is decision making a cognitive process?

For our purposes, we can think of *cognition* and *thinking* as synonyms. Entrepreneurs ask, "What are my resources? What's a course of action that I'd like to pursue? What are the results that I desire? What do I do as things change?".

As entrepreneurs, we always have choices. There are multiple alternatives at every stage. There is the option of not doing anything and waiting to see what happens. There's an element of choice that is implied with decision making.

Decision making is a strategic activity. As an entrepreneur, you will need to set your revenue goals and your profit goals, and create your marketing plans and hiring strategies. Every strategic decision is influenced by your own comfort level with the risk involved with that decision. Your personal mindset, motivations, and behaviors guide your decision making.

Strategic decisions demand critical analysis. They involve consideration of required resources and commitment levels, and expected risks and rewards.

Jeff Bezos, the founder of Amazon, introduced an incredible and lasting phenomenon with his company. Granted, it's easy to look at entrepreneurs after they have had success, and hear them tell you how right they were, how they made all the right decisions, and how they have had this wonderful success. It's rare to be able look at entrepreneurs who are successful before they became successful.

To see them fifteen or twenty years prior, when they were just beginning to build their success. What their decision making and thought processes were then, and what they expected to happen. And in that way, we have the benefit of understanding the future and knowing the future. We see what happened according to plan, and see what was modified, or adapted. Historic video interviews and articles can provide us with this retrospective lens, and we see that Jeff Bezos was an innovative, prophetic thinker from the start.

I invite you to view "The Jeff Bezos of 1999: Nerd of the

Amazon" on the CBS News website or elsewhere online. This provides a perspective on the world's richest person before he achieved the success known to us today.

Why study strategic decision making?

We all need to be better entrepreneurial decision makers. Through this book, we can understand what's different about the decision making of entrepreneurs versus typical managers. We also want to learn how to make more efficient and effective decisions with reasonable resource commitments and relative speed.

The environment of entrepreneurs is uniquely challenging. Entrepreneurs are, or at least should be, doing new things. They may not have all the resources and relationships of established companies. There are higher levels of uncertainty and complexity, and greater levels of consequences from failure. If you're a large firm, and you spend a million dollars for an undesirable outcome, that's probably recoverable. The consequences for entrepreneurs are more significant. As an entrepreneur, misspending several thousand dollars may result in the end of your company. Entrepreneurs are under more stress in making decisions.

Through effective decision making we can improve our clarity and focus. We can make better decisions, even with limited information. We can accept higher levels of risk that involve major consequences.

Many strategic decisions need to be made, and many considerations need to be taken into effect. Those decision-making elements are mental processes. They are cognitive processes as you look at opportunities, and think about skills and abilities, and how to navigate them. We will address:

- Studying the psychological traits of entrepreneurs, and

discussing how you can enhance these within yourself;

- Examining the opportunity discovery aspects of how to recognize and develop new ideas;
- Exploring the cognitive aspects of decision making, and really think about the thinking that goes in entrepreneurship; and
- Developing the analytical skills to evaluate and select opportunities.

Entrepreneurs make significant decisions in dynamic and uncertain environments. There are tools and techniques to facilitate making these decisions. My goal is to help you anticipate, analyze, and make better decisions in your entrepreneurial pursuits.

In summary, strategic decision making is certainly something that we're familiar with, whether we've called it that or not. We do it with frequency, professionally and personally. It's something that we need to better understand. And it's something that we can improve upon individually.

We also want to recognize that we can learn from others. We can learn from other entrepreneurs. We can learn from other successful companies and startups, and what they did for better and for worse, in the creation and growth of their ventures. We recognize that studying decision making is helpful to being better entrepreneurial decision makers and better entrepreneurs.

What is your decision-making style?

In the study of entrepreneurial decision making, it's very helpful to understand and recognize your personal decision-making style. In this book, we'll talk about how you can understand your personal preferences for decision making, and what you may do to enhance your decision-making style.

We will begin with a discussion on rationality. The rational decision maker is data driven. They make decisions based on logical analysis. They don't rely on their gut, or would prefer not to, particularly if it contradicts what they're finding in the facts.

Separate from rationality is intuition, of making decisions based on feelings and emotions. You may, in this case, avoid the facts. You may avoid the logical analysis if it contrasts with what your gut tells you.

When you ponder these two styles, consider whether you are rational or intuitive when it comes to significant decisions.

When you think about rational versus intuitive, I encourage you to put them into context and to think about past actions. Think about a career choice, a significant purchase, or your personal relationships. Were you rational or intuitive there? That's probably a good indicator of your preferred style, when you look at it historically and what you've done and why you've done it, and what role the rational or the intuitive played in that.

Are successful entrepreneurs rational or intuitive decision makers?

The short answer is "both". What we see with successful entrepreneurs is that most are rational and intuitive decision makers. In that way, when we look at the various elements of the startup venture, you can work to be rational, but you're never going to have all the data. You're never going to have all of the facts or answers of what to do. Inversely, you're not always operating in the dark. You're not always operating without information and without resources. So, you don't have to be entirely intuitive about everything. The challenge is that you have to recognize where you are, or where your preferences tend to be, and what you can do to augment that, and to raise your competency in both.

You can make decisions that are highly rational and highly intuitive. We'll talk about those in a few different contexts.

Concept development is certainly one; it should involve market research and a lot of gut feelings as well. It's that early ideation phase of what is the product? What's the benefit that you want to bring forth? It takes a lot of intuition.

Soon after that, there's the element of market analysis. Does anybody care? Is there a customer out there? Is it competitive with what's already in the market? And that's where we can integrate our analytical efforts.

You also need to understand where the market is headed, where your competitors are headed. And that takes you back to intuition. What do you think the feature set of your competitor is going to be six months from now?

We also want to recognize that customer discovery requires rational and intuitive decision making. Customers are difficult to understand, and their needs and wants change over time. There's the expectation that you're going to do research. But you're also going to do your own customer discovery and analysis, and apply your intuition.

Product design and prototyping requires vision and quantitative data. Communicate with team members, advisors, and other people who can challenge your thoughts, who can make suggestions, and who can help you evolve your ideas to better understand what your product should be. You also want to recognize the value of generating alternatives, of testing assumptions, gathering data, understanding what works and what doesn't work, and why people prefer certain things. Will they pay for that feature? And what will they pay?

You're always integrating the rational and the intuitive. Keep asking yourself, what information is missing? What can I add?

Fundraising tends to be quantitative. Investors ask, what are your revenues and expenses? How much funding do you need to raise, at what point, at what time, on what terms, and at what valuation? You cannot go to an investor with only your gut feeling. Nor should you do it to yourself. Fundraising is very numbers driven. But there's always a degree of intuition that's factored into how you do your estimates, what your expectations are, what your key assumptions are.

In summary, when we look at these elements of decision-making style, remember that entrepreneurs need to make relatively quick decisions with high stakes, and with incomplete information, in a dynamic market.

This isn't simply an exercise of "I am this way" or "I am that way." It's a journey of recognizing who you are, and what's your roadmap to enhancing those elements, and what you can do to improve your decision making and thereby improve your entrepreneurial success.

Chapter 4. Part I - Thinking Entrepreneurially

Entrepreneurial Mindset
Entrepreneurial Motivation
Entrepreneurial Behaviors

With an appreciation for the opportunities and challenges of strategic decision making, you can explore the next chapters on *entrepreneurial mindset, entrepreneurial motivation,* and *entrepreneurial behavior* as the first three steps of the Opportunity Analysis Canvas.

The Opportunity Analysis Canvas
Emphasis on "Part I – Thinking Entrepreneurially"

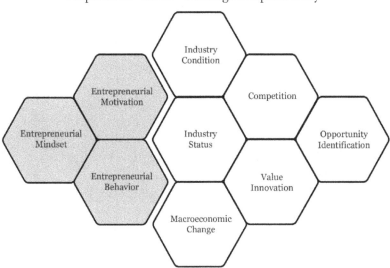

Chapter 5. Entrepreneurial Mindset

Part of the challenge of being an entrepreneur, if you're going for a really huge opportunity, is trying to find problems that aren't quite on the radar yet and try to solve those.

Sean Parker

Former President of Facebook and Co-founder of Napster

Why is the *entrepreneur* at the heart of *entrepreneur*ship?

While I will introduce the role of market opportunities, technology changes, and other factors in entrepreneurship, it is important to recognize that the person, the entrepreneur, is at the heart of the matter. This is why an understanding of the mindset of entrepreneurs is critical to understanding how to develop and launch successful ventures.

By exploring *entrepreneurial mindset*, you can understand why less than 5% of society become entrepreneurs. Entrepreneurs tend to be independent individuals, intensely committed to persevering in starting and growing a venture. They are typically optimists who strive for success in their for-profit, non-profit, or social venture. They often burn with the competitive desire to excel, and use failure not as a referendum, but as a learning tool.

While every entrepreneur is unique, there are select commonalities in entrepreneurial mindset that they share. This chapter focuses on that entrepreneurial mindset, with attention to the five characteristics: *achievement, individualism, control, focus,* and *optimism.*

The Opportunity Analysis Canvas
Emphasis on "Entrepreneurial Mindset"

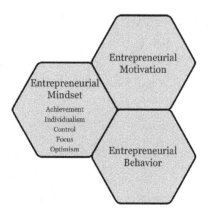

Do you have a high need for achievement?

Need for achievement is a preference for challenge coupled with an acceptance of personal responsibility for outcomes. A personal drive for accomplishment evidences one's need for achievement. We may call it drive. We may call it hunger. We may call it being a self-starter, or being self-motivated. All of those would be accurate as we think about need for achievement in this context.

What we see is that entrepreneurs typically have a higher need for achievement than managers. What we call a manager in this context is a corporate or government employee.

Need for achievement plays a key role in creating the entrepreneur. For individuals who score high in need for achievement, the likelihood of them becoming an entrepreneur is high.

A high need for achievement makes for better entrepreneurs. Naturally, if you have a greater motivation, a greater drive, and a greater level of commitment, you're going to have higher involvement in your job and in your career. You're going to have higher organizational commitment and commitment to colleagues, suppliers, partners, customers, and investors. Need for achievement is therefore an enabler of becoming a successful entrepreneur.

How do you know if you have a high need for achievement?

Take a step back and think about the entrepreneur. Think about yourself. We want to know what it means to have this need for achievement.

We first want to think about goal setting.

- Do you have personal goals?
- Are they written?
- Are they specific and challenging and relevant?
- Do you mentally rehearse or forecast or think about future events?
- Do you anticipate obstacles?
- Do you develop alternative solutions?
- And are you not only driven to success, but are you planning your own success?

Self-monitoring is something to keep in mind as well. Are you tracking progress towards your goals? I'm a believer in tracking what we care about, and measuring our progress towards our ambitions. Self-monitoring and milestone measuring are practices of individuals with a high need for achievement.

Self-reinforcement is important. Do you reward yourself for your achievement? Either with incremental rewards, or long-term rewards?

Are you self-motivated? Or do you need others to encourage you in order to feel motivated?

Do you need others to congratulate you? Or do you find satisfaction in your own success? Are you fulfilled without receiving the recognition of others?

Analyzing your own need for achievement is valuable to diagnosing and enhancing your level. We are all at different levels. And it's not to say that you are where you are and that's all there is to it. What we hope to do within each of these elements is identify and assess where we are, and work towards improving ourselves in each element.

In summary, need for achievement is a key component of the entrepreneurial mindset. It's one of the five key components that we're going to analyze. It's motivating for individuals to pursue their new venture's success, and contributory to their success as entrepreneurs.

How does individualism influence your decision making?

Individualism is a key element of the entrepreneurial mindset. When we define the term individualism, it means that you need less support or approval from others. You may place a very high value on independence, freedom, and control. There may be a willingness, even a preference, to go against the norm. High individualism is associated with an emphasis on individual initiative and a high need for achievement.

Collectivism is the alternative to individualism. As individuals, we focus on "I." If you're a collectivist, you focus on the "we."

Individuals have their own goals, while collectivists have group goals. Individualists emphasize themselves, while collectivists have a group emphasis.

With individualism, the element of reciprocity or sharing is not required, and may not even be preferred. With collectivism, reciprocity is expected.

Individualist manage individuals.

Collectivists manage the group.

When we examine individualism and collectivism, we are interested in their relevance to entrepreneurship and decision making. We'll deconstruct and think about this at the abstract and the concrete levels.

Individualism is tightly correlated with decision making based on achievement and risk taking. There's more assertiveness. There's more speed to action.

Inversely, when we look at collectivism, there's more sensitivity for the group. There's more consideration of developing the buy-in and the consensus of others. There's also a measure of security that's involved in making a safer decision. What that can mean is that collectivist mindset decisions are slower to come by. They're more complex with more viewpoints, more individuals, and perhaps other groups or organizations that play a role in the decision. You may even avoid decisions or simply agree to disagree on areas. You may potentially come up with the sub-optimum decision because you're trying to satisfy many different groups that may or may not have common interests.

Individualism and collectivism were historically viewed as exclusive categories, and people were believed to be one or the other. What we have realized as of late is that most people have a combination of both. While they may have a "we" identity and they are concerned about their group, they may preface their individual goals to those of others. They may have an individual emphasis in their decision making, but they still believe that reciprocity and sharing with the group is valuable.

What causes happiness?

Our national and ethnic cultures play a substantial role in our personal balance of individualism and collectivism. In collaboration with Gallup, a research-based, global performance-management consulting company, Columbia University recently did a study where they looked at the 40 happiest countries on earth. Denmark, Finland, Norway, the Netherlands, and Canada were the top five. Switzerland, Sweden, New Zealand, Australia, and Ireland rounded out the top ten.

What causes national happiness? Perhaps it's wealth, but if we correlate per capita gross domestic product (GDP), the financial wealth of a nation, with happiness, there is no relationship.

Perhaps it's life expectancy. With health and long life, there's happiness. Right? There's no correlation here, either. The higher life expectancy countries—Japan, Singapore, Hong Kong—are not among top 10 happiest countries.

Perhaps it's safety, but it's not. Only a few of the safest countries earn a place among the happiest countries.

What is the cause for this happiness? Research suggests that the happiest places tend to be collectivist countries instead of those with an individualist nature.

In summary, individualism and collectivism are relevant to your entrepreneurial success. Entrepreneurs tend to have a higher level of individualism, but too much may be detrimental. We do not benefit from entirely lacking this collectivism aspect. Once you understand your preferences between individualism and collectivism, you can strive towards developing a balance.

Do you believe that you have control of your own destiny?

In considering the question of your belief that you have *control* of your own destiny, we'll deconstruct the term into two pieces: *autonomy* and *locus of control*.

How does autonomy influence control of your own destiny?

With *autonomy*, we're considering your freedom from the influence of others in decisions that you make. For the significant decisions that you make, you may solicit advice and counsel, and consider others' inputs. But when it comes down to it, are you the number one influencer and the number one decision maker? And can you act on your decision, and what you think is right, with relative independence and freedom from the influence of others?

One way to think about autonomy in action is to consider your perspectives on a job. Is a job primarily for your economic security? Is it comfortable? Is it a source of satisfaction? Or, does it prohibit you from reaching your ultimate goals? Is it constraining? And is entrepreneurship a way to tackle that, and a way to free yourself from a job?

In my experience, the idea that entrepreneurship provides you with total autonomy and total freedom is a fallacy. Your old bosses are not removed, but replaced. If you start your own company, you may not have a boss in a traditional sense, but you have customers, partners, and investors, all of whom have a certain level of expectation, demand, or influence. Your 9-to-5 working hours are now 24 hours a day. And your new work week? Well, it may have been Monday through Friday in the past. As an entrepreneur, particularly in the early days of the venture, it may be 7 days per week. There are long days, there are short days. There are pieces of days that are segmented over that 24 hour period, that if you don't do the work, it doesn't get done. You do control how you do your work. You have relatively unbounded influence and flexibility. You can decide the level of freedom for yourself that still allows you to deliver value to your customers, partners, and investors.

Based on a recent *Inc. 500* survey, the typical entrepreneur starts their day at 6:30 am. They may work, at the beginning of the day, for an hour or so. They may then have a commute to an office or co-working space. During the drive, train ride, subway transit, or whatever their form of transportation, half of them are doing work during their commute. There is meeting time throughout the day, which may be meeting with your team, if you're already at the point of having a team. Or it may be meeting with customers or prospective partners or investors. This may take an hour or two a day. Then there's a mix of activity of communicating with other partners and colleagues. Emailing alone consumes approximately two hours a day for the typical entrepreneur. Lunch breaks are taken by approximately one-third of entrepreneurs. Others work as they can, and eat as they can on the go. There's an afternoon break at 5:00 pm when traditionally individuals may be accustomed to stopping work for the day. We need time for exercise and/or family time. We see a return to work after dinner, and perhaps relaxation time later as well. The average bedtime is 10:30 pm based on that waking time of 6:30 am.

What this illustrates is that as an entrepreneur it's a busy day and it can be a long day, but there can still be time for family and friends. While the element of working 24 hours a day is not necessarily there, entrepreneurs rarely work a 9-to-5 schedule, particularly in the early years of the startup.

The element of complete autonomy and complete freedom for entrepreneurs, while a fallacy, does deliver the opportunity to be flexible and dynamic, and to do things on times that suit you, how you want them done, and increasingly, where you want them done.

How does locus of control influence control of your own destiny?

The second element that we'll examine is the *locus of control*, which is a different side of control that looks at the individual's belief that they can influence others, or that they can influence the environment.

When good things happen, do you attribute that to what you did, or to what happened externally? Inversely, when bad things happen, do you take accountability for that? Do you take control of that situation, or do you attribute that to others?

Locus of control is either internally or externally oriented. Locus of control that's internally oriented means that you believe, as an individual, that you are in control and able to influence your environment and its outcomes. Inversely, externally oriented means that you're feeling subject to people and events, that you have minimal influence. You attribute fate or luck or other external factors to what caused certain things to happen.

Individuals who have higher levels of internal locus of control drive entrepreneurial opportunity discovery and action at a higher rate than those with an external locus of control. When you believe you have a measure of influence and you can make something happen, even if the economy, or the government, or competitors are not necessarily in your favor, you have a greater likelihood of bringing about entrepreneurial change than those who believe they are subject to an external locus of control. The element of creating your own destiny is in large part based on your belief of having this internal locus of control.

For illustration, imagine that you are interested in starting a new payment processing company. You believe that you can compete with American Express, Visa, and MasterCard for online payment processing. You think that you can change the way that customers buy products online. You start PayPal.

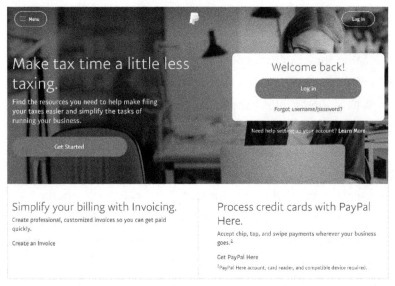

Figure 3. Paypal Website

Next, you set your sights on competing against the world's largest automotive manufacturers. You believe that you have a new way to build, sell, and service cars. You desire to fundamentally change the technology as well as the dealership model for sales and service. You eventually accomplish this, while elevating the driving experience and customer satisfaction, while reducing the harmful emissions of gasoline-based automobiles. You started Tesla.

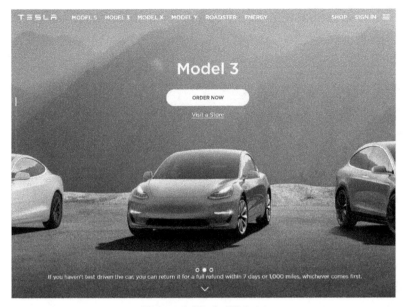

Figure 4. Tesla Website

As a founder of PayPal and Tesla, Elon Musk epitomizes the entrepreneur's internal locus of control.

Do you believe that you have the ability to successfully pursue that opportunity? That's where autonomy and locus of control play a role in your ability to execute on these beliefs. This depends on the degree to which you believe that you can influence others, the environment, and the circumstances that exist.

In summary, beliefs about the value of entrepreneurial opportunities are driven by the individual, and their willingness to take action on their ideas. The ability to make an idea a reality is in large part based on how you operate in the sense of how independently you operate.

Are you able to effectively focus your time and resources?

With competing interests and dynamic priorities, *focus* is a central challenge for entrepreneurs. Developing an ability to focus our time and energy is an important step to enhancing our entrepreneurial mindset.

Our definition of focus in this context is concentration on a specific issue or task. To really focus, you need self-discipline and motivation. Do you have the commitment and attention span to see a task through to completion with high quality and relative speed?

Successful entrepreneurs can focus on a task and see it through to completion, or see it through to its next milestone. We can be more efficient, and do things better, by giving it our full attention, by processing information efficiently and thoroughly. This enables us to be decisive and thoughtful in our decisions

As an experiment, detach yourself from email, at least in part, for a day. Check it three times: once in the morning, near noon, and late in the day. During those times, reply to your emails as desired, and send emails as needed. If something urgent happens in the interim, you will likely receive a phone call. At the end of the day, consider if you were more productive with this abbreviated email schedule versus your normal day of regular email monitoring.

As a second experiment, reduce your use of the phone. Allow your voicemail to answer all non-critical calls. Set aside one time during the day to return calls, perhaps near the end of the day.

By reducing interruptions of our work, our focus and productivity skyrockets.

To assist with your focus, I suggest using timelines for your tasks and goals. Create a plan for what you want to achieve by what time or day. With your timeline, particularly your daily timelines and to-do lists, be sure to schedule breaks and vary your tasks as possible. As the human attention span typically declines after two hours, taking short periodic breaks can be more productive than being heads down and staring at a computer all day.

I suggest that you maintain a to-do list that you actually schedule on your calendar. You should know how much time you're going to spend each day on various tasks. That allows you to structure your day and to have time allotments, and forces you to adopt a principal of "done is better than perfect." That way you're bringing things to a close, and you're able to make progress on the next task.

I also encourage you to be goal-oriented, and think about the outcome of what you're doing, and how you measure that outcome. Writing down your goals is valuable in clarifying and quantifying what you're trying to achieve. Putting a timeline to your goals improves your likelihood of actually getting there. And you need to reward yourself as you have success, as you reach these goals and milestones. Take time, go to dinner, go on a vacation, buy an item, give a gift—these are things that entrepreneurs are certainly allowed to do and that I would encourage you to do. That way you see some of that material success, and you reap satisfaction as you go.

Communicating with fellow aspiring and active entrepreneurs is valuable to focusing your time and energy. Talking with those of similar ambitions with similar struggles reduces the sense of isolation and hopelessness that we may experience as entrepreneurs. It's also inspirational to see the successes of others.

Meditation, prayer, and other methods of embracing calm and peace further assist in developing your focus. Turn things off and sit quietly for a time to reflect on your goals and interests.

As you begin to grow your venture and engage with others, you will become a better leader. A primary task of leadership is directing your attention towards the goal, and being able to focus the attention of your team. Think about how things happen, what you can do to motivate them to happen, and how to focus on the big picture.

Leaders need to cultivate awareness. That includes inward focus, a focus on others, and outward focus. Inward focus and the focus on others are related to emotional intelligence. Daniel Goleman's book, *Emotional Intelligence*, is valuable to understanding these principles. Outward focus enables you to improve your ability to devise strategies, innovate, and manage the organization.

"A wealth of information creates a poverty of attention," said economist Herbert Simon in 1971. This is a prophetic statement, given that it was written over forty years ago. What we see today, particularly as entrepreneurs, is an immense flood of information and data. How do we act on this? What do we focus on? What do we give our attention to? Developing the ability to effectively focus your time and resources is an asset for entrepreneurs.

Do friends characterize you as an optimist?

In our consideration of *optimism*, I framed this question differently to change the point of reference. While most of the traits that we're exploring can be self-assessed effectively, your optimism is better measured by how other people see you.

A textbook definition for being optimistic is to anticipate the best possible result. The optimum result. We'll modify this definition to include a "favorable" outcome that may not be the optimum result. While the optimum result may not occur, if you're an optimist, you do expect that the outcome will be at least favorable.

Does optimism truly improve performance?

Yes, and it's evidenced in multiple studies.

Metropolitan Life Insurance Company was the subject of a study where the sales agents who were more optimistic sold dramatically more than those who were pessimistic. The more optimistic half of sales agents in the study sold 37% more than the pessimistic half. The most optimistic 10% of sales agents sold 88% more than the most pessimistic 10% of sales agents.

The United States Military Academy at West Point studied optimism as an indicator of graduation. They found that optimism was a greater influencer of a cadet's likelihood of graduating from the university than SAT scores or high school grades.

In the U.S. professional baseball (MLB) and basketball (NBA) associations, athletes who scored higher in optimism evaluations experienced more success in their athletic careers

In professional, academic, and athletic settings, we see that optimism matters, and those who are optimistic perform at a higher level.

There are benefits to optimism. It encourages entrepreneurs to try new things. It enables entrepreneurs to attempt the difficult, and attempt things that they may feel they don't have the right education or experience for, but they're willing to try anyway. We think that we can have a favorable outcome, and we'll make a go of it as entrepreneurs if we have an optimistic outlook.

Optimism can also be contagious. If we're optimistic, it tends to influence our team to be optimistic, as well as our partners and our investors to share in our enthusiasm and excitement.

It's important to note that there are cons to being overly optimistic. We may overlook critical elements because we want to dive right in. We may discount uncertainties. Were we to do more research and analysis, we would be better prepared. If we are overly optimistic, we'll accept undue levels of risk. This can contribute to excessive business losses or complete failure of the venture. While I champion being optimistic, I do not discourage your being research-driven and strategy-minded.

There is also a bias to be aware of. Most of us underestimate our chances of divorce or losing a job or having disease. We overestimate the likelihood of our children being academically gifted, of what level of wealth we will achieve, and how long we will live. To learn more, I encourage you to view the TED talk titled The Optimism Bias at ted.com.

We should seek balanced optimism. With that balance, we want to think about the relative costs of pessimism versus the benefits of optimism. We want to recognize the importance of balance in understanding the relative levels of powers and influence. And we want to think about, how do you do that? How do you get on this balanced path?

Can optimism be learned?

Optimism can certainly be learned, according to Martin Seligman, the author of *Learned Optimism*. Let's highlight the principles and takeaways that he suggests for learning to be more optimistic.

1. The first step is to learn to identify situations and events that we routinely face. To document them and to think about the challenges that we encounter.
2. Then write your beliefs and assumptions. What comes to mind? What do we expect? Can we separate the facts from our feelings, and have a more objective view and objective account of what it is that we're facing.
3. The third step is to think about consequences and the levels of emotions and energy, and what's happening and what we did.
4. Then think about the elements that you may dispute. There may be a devil's advocate way of thinking about what else may have happened, what may we have missed, what else could have influenced this? We look at evidence. We think about alternatives and consider other implications. Again, documenting these elements.
5. Lastly, we think about the level of influence of energy and beliefs over time. We think about how these elements of emotions and feelings, be they of a pessimistic or of an optimistic nature, have influenced the decisions that we've made. Have we encountered an initial hurdle, but because we felt that it was difficult, we stopped? Or have we performed at somewhat of a lackluster level? Or conversely, if we thought that it was difficult, but we gave it our full energy anyway, what was the outcome then?

This five-step approach is a way of establishing and developing optimism. We can also better understand the root causes of our pessimism.

A number of the characteristics and behaviors that we've discussed are influenced by our experiences. We have the capacity to learn things as individuals, to unlearn, and to relearn. And that's true of emotional behaviors and psychological patterns. In that sense, when we begin to understand who we are and what we are, it gives us the opportunity to enhance and redevelop ourselves.

In summary, the optimistic approach combined with high reality testing is the ideal balance. We avoid being overly optimistic. We don't want to fool ourselves into thinking we should do things that we haven't analyzed. We do want to focus on positive options, and become an *"optionist"* in the context of thinking about how to move forward and how to be optimistic as entrepreneurs. Also within this element, we want to emphasize our capacity to learn, to unlearn, and to relearn. And that's true of optimism and the other factors that we've been discussing.

Entrepreneur Spotlight on Anthony Casalena, Founder and CEO of Squarespace

As with Dell, Facebook, and countless technology startups, Squarespace was hatched in a college dorm. Anthony Casalena developed the vision for this leading web development platform when he was a junior at the University of Maryland in 2003.

A project to make a personal website was the result of his dissatisfaction with existing services. Anthony recalls, "At the time, you had to seek out and cobble together a mix of blogging software, statistics software, page builder software, and web hosting. Instead of going that route, I decided to create an elegant solution that offered all the necessary elements to build a professional website. Further, none of the hosting or publishing services available really had a focus on design. I wasn't comfortable using them for my online identity."[7]

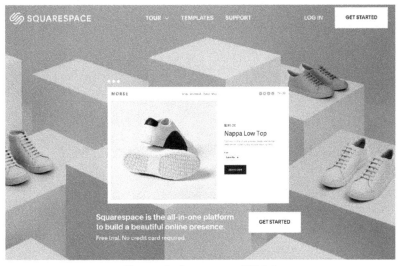

Figure 5. Squarespace Website

---

[7] Johnston, M. (2013). "Interview with Squarespace CEO and Founder, Anthony Casalena." April 22, 2013. www.cmscritic.com

His solution was to build his own tool for creating professional, feature-rich, esthetically attractive websites. In solving his own problem, he realized that others shared his plight. Customers joined for $8 per month, and a first place win in the University of Maryland's Business Plan Competition followed.

By focusing his time and resources on building the best solution possible, and by believing that he could build not only a great product but a great company, Squarespace became a leader in its industry. With $300 million in annual sales[8], the company is listed among *Forbes'* "America's Most Promising Companies," *Time'*s "50 Best Websites," and *Inc. 500'*s list of "America's Fastest Growing Companies" for three consecutive years.

---

[8] Dickey, M.R. (2017) "Squarespace reportedly raises about $200 million at a $1.7 billion valuation." December 14, 2017. www.techcrunch.com

Ideas in Action: The Entrepreneurial Mindset

With your awareness of the opportunities and challenges of strategic decision making, this activity challenges you to explore your entrepreneurial mindset as the first step of the Opportunity Analysis Canvas.

To facilitate your self-reflection, please discuss your entrepreneurial mindset by answering each of these questions. Your answers should be personalized based on your own experiences and perspectives.

What role does need for achievement play in your decisions?	
What level of influence do friends and family have in your decision making?	

Do you have an internal or external locus of control?	
What techniques do you use to focus your time and resources?	
How can you improve your level of optimism?	

Chapter 6. Entrepreneurial Motivation

Motivation is everything. You can do the work of two people, but you can't be two people. Instead, you have to inspire the next guy down the line and have him to inspire his people.

Lee Iacocca

Past President and CEO of Chrysler

Entrepreneurial motivation encompasses the factors by which goal-directed behavior is initiated, energized, and maintained. For entrepreneurial strategic decision making, three factors are emphasized: *self-efficacy, cognitive motivation,* and *tolerance for ambiguity.*

The Opportunity Analysis Canvas
Emphasis on "Entrepreneurial Motivation"

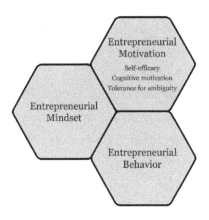

Do you have high self-efficacy?

As we turn our attention to *entrepreneurial motivation*, we're going to start the conversation with a discussion of *self-efficacy*. Specifically, we'll examine how self-efficacy impacts you and your motivations, and how to improve your personal self-efficacy.

Self-efficacy is your belief in your ability to accomplish a specific task. It intersects an element of mindset, as well as an element of entrepreneurial motivation.

Richard Branson's creation of over 400 companies, to include a number that are global leaders, personifies entrepreneurial self-efficacy. He demonstrates his belief that he can be effective in creating, launching, and growing new ventures.

Self-efficacy may sound like confidence, but it differs. Confidence is a general characteristic that applies to all tasks. We generally think of ourselves as being a confident person or an unconfident person.

Self-efficacy differs from confidence in that self-efficacy is task dependent. For example, if you enjoy numbers, you think of yourself as a numbers person, your self-efficacy for dealing with financial matters is probably high. If you fear public speaking, and you don't think you are effective as a public speaker, your self-efficacy for selling in front of an audience or marketing in front of a crowd may be low. For this person, who may be generally confident, their self-efficacy is high in finance and low in sales and marketing.

Sports presents another example of the difference between confidence and self-efficacy. You may feel that you're a generally confident person. However, if you've never played tennis, you may not feel that you're going to be very effective in your first attempt as a tennis player. Your self-efficacy for playing tennis is low, although you are still a generally confident person.

The benefits of having a high self-efficacy as it's related to entrepreneurship are many. It certainly is a key predictor of individual performance. Naturally, if you think that you can do something well, like our discussion of optimism, the likelihood of actually doing it well is higher than if you go into it with a low self-efficacy. For that reason it's valuable to increase our self-efficacy.

This is a short story of a small, family-owned billboard company outside of Atlanta, Georgia. The father of the company passed away when the son was 25 years old. The son built the company up over the subsequent years into a large billboard and advertising business. He then became involved and interested in television, and bought a small, local Atlanta station. This was in the 1970s. When you own a television station, you need content. If you want to make maximum use of your channel that you've purchased and are broadcasting on, you need 24 hours of content, seven days a week. One way to do that is to produce shows and movies, but that's expensive. Another way to do that is to buy content from others, but that's expensive, too. Given the relative youth and limited success of the Atlanta Braves baseball team, they were an affordable option to buying content for the television station. Subsequently, professional wrestling fit the same mold. This entrepreneur went from billboard promoter to television broadcaster to sports owner. That then brought him back full circle into thinking about advertising and television. At the time, broadcasting 24-hour news seven days a week was not considered a smart idea by most people in the industry. If it had been a good idea, you'd think that NBC, ABC, CBS, the BBC, and other leading television broadcasters around the globe would have done it. CNN was the first to do news 24/7. That has blossomed into many other channels that you're likely familiar with. More recently, this same entrepreneur's gone into restaurants.

If you haven't figured it out by now, I'm talking about Ted Turner and the success that he's had in the context of having a very high self-efficacy as it's related to business, and as it's related to starting and growing a variety of different types and categories of businesses that are very different, from advertising, to media, to sports, to restaurants. He's had great success in many of these, but he's had faults. He had one fault in a merger that caused him to lose 80% of his wealth, yet he is still a billionaire.

In summary, when we examine self-efficacy, it is a key predictor of individual performance in entrepreneurial endeavors. Now, for some of us it may be innate. For others it may be learned. For all of us, it can be improved. There are elements of our background, experiences, childhood, professional experiences, and education that influence our self-efficacy. Learning how to improve self-efficacy starts with understanding the principle, and focusing on improving for the future.

Do you exhibit high cognitive motivation?

In our discussion of *cognitive motivation*, we'll examine its role as an entrepreneurial motivator. We will also explore its impacts on the success entrepreneurs, and how you can improve your own cognitive motivation. This is the second element that we're exploring within the topic of entrepreneurial motivation.

When we consider the term cognitive, fundamentally it's the process of thought. When adding motivation to this term, we're addressing the question of do you enjoy problem solving? And do you use research and analysis to solve problems?

Individuals with high cognitive motivation tend to seek, acquire, and analyze information. They're researchers. They're analytics.

Individuals with low cognitive motivation typically rely on their experience, intuition, assumptions, and luck.

Eric Knight, the author of *Reframe*, explores cognitive motivation in the context of problem solving, and what's involved in rethinking and reframing problems on a path to developing innovative and highly effective solutions.

High cognitive motivation aligns with activities that we process in our left-brain. Information search and processing is a primary activity. Those with high cognitive motivation seek the details. They often move in a sequential order and use logic to solve problems.

Alternatively, individuals with lower cognitive motivation, the right-brained, typically think holistically. They may see the big picture and have an end result in mind. They're creative in their pursuit of problem solving, in that tasks appear random, and intuition is a key tool for their problem solving.

Solving problems via a high cognition or low cognition approach can both yield positive solutions. In entrepreneurship, the problems are often ill defined and the information is often lacking. Decisions may be relatively unprecedented. Entrepreneurs need to exercise both their left brain and right brain in problem solving.

How can we improve the classroom experience?

By illustration, in America's classrooms we're trying to solve the problem of how do you better educate students, have better outcomes, have a more engaging experience, improve retention, and produce better graduates.

Integrating technology into the classroom experience is a popular approach today. Teachers generally appreciate the value of using technology to support diverse learning styles among students, and to create a more motivating environment by enhancing the material being taught.

Online courses also present a unique and novel way to learn dynamically, and to learn in a semi-customized fashion.

Gamification and social learning online are emerging techniques as well.

We see technology in the context of mobile apps, and tablets not only for homework, but also in the classroom. We also see more eBooks, digital textbooks, and open source digital books.

Learning analytics helps teachers assess the concerns and achievements of students. Teachers can monitor in real time how students are performing on tasks that are done within the class, and can attend to a specific student who may be having a specific problem. Teachers can provide personal, real-time attention rather than waiting till the end of the week or till the end of the semester to discover that a student was having problems with a certain concept.

There are also non-technology innovations emerging in classrooms at the K-12 and college levels. There is an increase in problem-based learning and project-based learning. The context of the teaching is tied to real-world problems. Real problems with companies and organizations are brought into the classroom, and may include class visits from company representatives.

There's a broad question of how we employ technology, online courses, devices, social networks, eBooks, learning analytics, etc. into a comprehensive solution for students that improves the quality and affordability of education. It's a hard problem that requires high cognitive motivation to solve.

What are the benefits of high cognitive motivation?

Individuals who have a higher need for cognitive motivation typically make better entrepreneurial decisions. If you don't like hard problems, if you expect to find the answers easily, or if you expect to have lots of precedence, then entrepreneurship is a hard way to go. If, however, you enjoy the challenge, you enjoy difficult problems, and you enjoy trying to make a puzzle fit even though you may be missing pieces, that's more aligned with the entrepreneurial path.

Individuals who have a higher need for cognition are able to recall information and connect information in different ways. They're more accurate in analyzing that information, of thinking about arguments, counter arguments, alternative solutions, and the selection of solutions within that path. They demonstrate better logical reasoning along the way. Intuition and emotion play roles, but more attention is paid to the analytics of it and the logical decisions of it.

In summary, when we think about cognitive motivation, I encourage you to pursue a high cognition approach of being detail-oriented and research driven in your problem solving, while leveraging the left brain elements of creativity and a holistic perspective.

What is your tolerance for ambiguity?

As entrepreneurs face many dynamic challenges, *tolerance for ambiguity* is surely an asset. We'll examine tolerance for ambiguity in the context of entrepreneurship, its impact and influence on successful new venturing, as well as how to assess your personal tolerance for ambiguity. This is the third element of our discussion of entrepreneurial motivation as it relates to strategic decision making.

Our definition of tolerance for ambiguity is the tendency to perceive ambiguous or unclear situations as acceptable, or even desirable, rather than threatening.

The need for tolerance for ambiguity in entrepreneurship is clear, because markets change, customers change, competition changes, regulations change, and politics change. When you're dealing with many different changing forces, you need to be comfortable with experiencing the unexpected. And with that, you can make complex decisions relatively quickly with limited information.

By illustration, we can examine a public company, an entrepreneurial company, but a large company that has had to improve their tolerance for ambiguity. It had to respond to change and has had struggles of late. This is a company that I expect we all know well.

In a two-year span from 2006 to 2008, 80% of their market value disappeared. They went from a $40 stock to an $8 stock. Since then, they've rebounded under the guidance of their former CEO who returned to the company to guide its next chapter.

While not the founder of Starbucks, Howard Schultz was a very early entrant with the company and built it to be the global powerhouse that it is. One of the first things he did when he came back on board was to close every store in the U.S., all 7,100 stores, for three and a half hours, to retrain all of the baristas, all of the individuals that make the drinks. They found that the drinks were not consistently made to the quality that they desired, nor with the speed that was necessary. Customers were waiting in line for a long time to have a drink that they were unhappy with. To be, perhaps, unhappy enough not to return, or to voice discontent in having to remake their order or refund their purchase. This temporary closing may not seem like a big deal, but in just that three and a half hours, projections are that Starbucks lost $6 million in the U.S.; but it was necessary and fundamental to reframing the situation they were in.

They also redesigned many of their stores to return them back to a classic coffee house feel. They reduced the amount of non-food and non-drink merchandise. They reduced the floor displays of CDs, books, and merchandise that were overpowering the stores.

They also realized that while people knew them, they wanted them to have a greater mindshare of Starbucks. For the first time ever, they launched a national advertising campaign, print and television, to reintroduce Starbucks.

They kept things that were important to them, including health insurance. Starbucks is one of the only large companies in the U.S. that provide health insurance universally to all employees, including part-time employees. They could have saved significant costs, hundreds of millions of dollars, by reducing that or doing away with it, but they chose not to. They saw this support of employee welfare, well-being, and health as critical to what they were as a company. They've held onto those values even in challenging times, even as the voice of many stockholders suggested that they reduce health benefits expenses. They've had the courage not to do that, and to do other new things.

One of them is instant coffee, which for decades has been viewed as the lowest of the lowest quality of coffee—something that was bought in grocery stores for several dollars per jar, or 20 cents per serving. Starbucks brought their instant coffee to market at $1 per serving. They've aimed to do it at very high quality, and have put in significant research and development and consumer testing to try and deliver a great instant product. They've done it, and they've done it well. They sell it in their stores as well as in groceries.

Starbucks also has a campaign by which they solicit customer ideas. Over the last five years, they've launched 277 customer-generated ideas. Things like free Wi-Fi—you would think to be obvious. But for many years, unless you were an AT&T customer, you could not have free Wi-Fi at Starbucks. That changed a few years ago. Customers have also brought to bear new flavor ideas, free birthday treats, happy hour, mobile payments, drive-thru service, cake pops, and a variety of other things. All under the concept of recognizing that they're in a changing and competitive global market. They're willing to listen to the customer to help reduce ambiguity and bring inspiring ideas to market.

Innovating, trying new things, and not being comfortable as they once were will serve Starbucks well. They've seen that if you're comfortable with the status quo, and stop innovating, you can lose 80% of your company value.

How can you improve your tolerance for ambiguity?

To understand your own tolerance for ambiguity, consider your comfort with uncertainty, with change, and with unfamiliar situations. Think about how you can improve your tolerance through experience. As you experience new things, the next time that you experience them, they're not new. You have new know-how. You have new capabilities that you've established. You have new insights, new relationships, and new resource for next time. Trying new things beyond your comfort zone, professionally and personally, is a good way to develop your tolerance for ambiguity.

It's also helpful to talk with aspiring and active entrepreneurs about their challenges. It demystifies the entrepreneurial experience. It makes starting a new venture less lonely. It emphasizes that you're not the only one facing challenges. Within cities and regions that you're residing, there may be networks of entrepreneurs that meet periodically—perhaps socially, perhaps professionally. You can talk, share stories, share solutions, and learn from others—and thereby improve your tolerance in that context as well.

In summary, when we think about tolerance for ambiguity, it's an asset to making decisions and making complex decisions quickly and with limited information. Uncertainty, change, and the unfamiliar are the norm when you're truly innovative. It's only in trying new things, and building relationships with others—particularly with fellow entrepreneurs—that makes navigating the ambiguous entrepreneurial journey more comfortable.

Entrepreneur Spotlight on Tony Hsieh,
Founder of LinkExchange and CEO of Zappos

In 1996, three 23 year-old college friends created LinkExchange. It quickly grew to prominence in the Internet advertising space, and in 1998 was sold to Microsoft for $265 million.

Financially, Tony Hsieh never had to work again. Driven by a need for new challenges, he invested most of his $30 million into his VentureFrogs startup incubator, which invested in Zappos.

This introduction to Zappos, an emerging online shoe retailer, as an advisor and investor occurred when the company had practically zero sales.

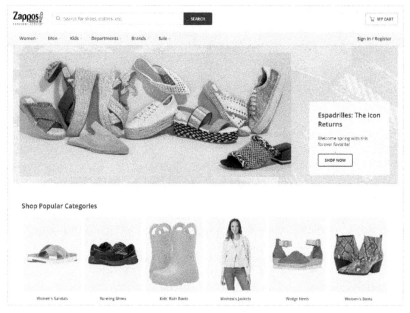

Figure 6. Zappos Website

Tony Hsieh believed that he could lead the firm to success in the hyper-competitive online apparel retail space, and invested his time and money to navigating the ambiguity ahead. He eventually became CEO of the company and grew sales to $1 billion annually. The company made *Fortune* magazine's annual "Best Companies to Work For" list, and in 2009, Zappos was acquired by Amazon.com for $1.2 billion.

What came next for Tony Hsieh, now with $840 million of personal wealth? Today, he marches on as Zappos' CEO, seeking new challenges and growth opportunities for the company. He continues to see new ways to excite customers and energize his employees. This is driven by his mantra of "powered by service," evidenced through Zappos' ten core values:[9]

1. Deliver WOW Through Service
2. Embrace and Drive Change
3. Create Fun and a Little Weirdness
4. Be Adventurous, Creative, and Open-Minded
5. Pursue Growth and Learning
6. Build Open and Honest Relationships With Communication
7. Build a Positive Team and Family Spirit
8. Do More With Less
9. Be Passionate and Determined
10. Be Humble

---

[9] Zappos (2013). Zappos Family Core Values. Zappos Corporate Website. http://about.zappos.com/our-unique-culture/zappos-core-values.

Ideas in Action: Entrepreneurial Motivation

With your awareness of the opportunities and challenges of strategic decision making, this activity challenges you to explore your entrepreneurial motivation as the second step of the Opportunity Analysis Canvas.

To facilitate your self-reflection, please discuss your entrepreneurial motivation by answering each of these questions. Your answers should be personalized based on your own experiences and perspectives.

Do you believe that you have the capabilities to be successful as an entrepreneur?	
Do you enjoy collecting information and doing analysis before making decisions?	

How can you increase
your comfort level
with making strategic
decisions quickly, with
limited information
and high
consequences?

Chapter 7. Entrepreneurial Behavior

Surround yourself only with people who are going to lift you higher.
Oprah Winfrey
Media proprietor, actress, producer, and philanthropist

Entrepreneurial mindset and motivation can only translate into action if *entrepreneurial behaviors* exist. While there are many behaviors that may be described as entrepreneurial, we'll focus on the four behaviors most critical to entrepreneurial opportunity analysis and action: *confidence, risk, interpersonal skills,* and *social capital.*

The Opportunity Analysis Canvas
Emphasis on "Entrepreneurial Behavior"

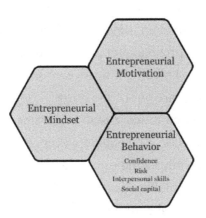

Do you have the confidence to attempt the difficult?

There are many statistics on the failure rates of startups. You may hear that 10% of new companies survive. Perhaps it's a 20% survival rate for second-time entrepreneurs. For entrepreneurs who have raised venture capital for their startups in the past, their success rate on future ventures may be 30%.

While the statistics are debatable, we recognize that in a startup, nothing is going to happen unless the entrepreneur tries to make it happen.

When we examine *confidence*, it's the belief in oneself or one's powers or abilities. Self-confidence, self-reliance, and self-assurance are related concepts. Confidence differs from self-efficacy in that self-efficacy relates to an individual activity. Confidence is a broader measure that generally applies to all tasks.

While we're aware of self-confidence as a concept, we may be unfamiliar with the signs of low self-confidence. Shy body language, a hesitancy to speak up, and avoiding interaction are overt signs of low self-confidence. Internal signs are being indecisive, fearing failure, resisting trust, and seeking external validation for our actions.

Entrepreneurs need to have confidence in their own judgment, particularly when things are difficult or when decisions are unpopular. Entrepreneurial opportunity discovery is constrained if there's limited confidence or discomfort with making decisions that are out of the norm.

In summary, self-confidence is an important tool within entrepreneurial behavior. You will miss every opportunity that you don't try. And while taking the advice of others, or going with the mainstream thinking, is the popular and easy thing to do, a high degree of personal confidence is required to be innovative.

Your confidence is critical to influencing others to participate in your startup as an investor, employee, partner, or customer. You need a high level of confidence when talking with investors, for recruiting prospective partners or co-founders, for bringing employees on board, and for communicating your product's benefits to customers.

What is your risk tolerance?

Risk is a concept that's commonly discussed in startup conversations. We're going to talk about the impact of *risk tolerance* on the success of new ventures.

To define risk in our context, it's the potential for loss. It's loss of money. It's loss of time.

There is also a risk in losing entrepreneurial opportunities. While loss of opportunity is a subjective assessment, the decision not to start a venture, or not launch a product, is a decision that involves risk of lost profit or lost success.

Do entrepreneurs prefer risk?

Do entrepreneurs by definition show a higher natural tendency to take risk? The short answer is "no." There's no significant difference between the risk tolerance of entrepreneurs and non-entrepreneurs. Non-entrepreneurs being those individuals that are working within corporations or established organizations.

Why do select individuals pursue new ventures? What's different about the risk that they see versus non-entrepreneurs? We all see risk differently. Our perceptions differ, and the risk perceptions differ between entrepreneurs and non-entrepreneurs. We may have a common risk tolerance, but what we see as risky differs. Risk is in the eye of the beholder. It's conceptualized based on our own assessment of the uncertainty, and our own consideration of the benefits and costs of an opportunity.

If you're seeking a high income, if you're seeking significant freedom over how you spend your time, if you're seeking high autonomy or control over products or services, you're probably not going to have that within an established company. And if you do, it's probably going to be years or decades away. That wait and hope may be a risky proposition.

If you're seeking a reliable income, if you're seeking a well-defined product or customer, and desire job security, you're probably not going to find that in startups. A startup would be risky if those are the goals that you're guided by.

If you want to have the opportunity for significant income, if you want to have reasonable flexibility, and autonomy, and control, then a startup could be a good fit. A startup would actually be a less risky proposition to pursue those elements than would a traditional employment relationship. It all depends on your goals, your perception of risk, and your assessment of the benefits and costs associated with a startup.

What do venture capitalists avoid?

While the failure rate of startups is difficult to accurately measure, we do know that of the startups that raise money from venture capitalists, over 80% survive. Survive does not necessarily mean that they are wildly successful or grow to millions of dollars in revenues. It simply means that they operate for more than five years as a company.

Why is the survival rate of venture-funded startups dramatically higher than startups without venture capital funding? If you can secure sufficient financial capital to create and launch your venture, and bring a product to market to generate sales for the company, your probability of success increases significantly.

A second reason for the success of venture-funded companies is buy-in. In order to secure funding, you've had to convince those early investors that you have a concept that's worth funding. They've bought in on your concept and your team to the point that they're willing to put in money. Not only is the money there, but there's also a validation by professional investors in startups that you have an idea with great potential.

Even if you do not plan to pursue investment from venture capitalist, it's valuable to note the types of firms that venture capital don't invest in, and how risk tolerance influences their decision making.

Venture capitalists typically avoid restaurants. Restaurants are problematic for venture capitalists for a number of reasons. One is a very high failure rate of up to 60%. Another is very high capital costs that are in large part unrecoverable. By the time you pay a lease, do renovations, hire a staff, do a reasonable amount of marketing, buy food—all of those are large, unrecoverable costs. Hundreds of thousands, perhaps even millions of dollars are invested before you open the doors to see if any customers are interested in your offering.

Retail stores are also commonly avoided by venture capitalists. Eighty percent of new retail stores close within the first five years. Why? It's a question of limited uniqueness and low barriers to entry. If you're selling products developed elsewhere, and those same products are available in other places, there's no uniqueness with your products. Your uniqueness may be limited to your location or additional services you can provide. A further challenge with retail is online competitors. It's difficult to successfully compete selling the products of others face-to-face if those products are also available online, and often at a lower price.

If restaurants, bricks-and-mortar retailers, and other minimally-differentiated businesses are removed from the startup failure rate equation, the success rates of startups dramatically improve. This is why I encourage you to seek entrepreneurial opportunities that are innovative and differentiated.

How can entrepreneurs minimize their risk?

Successful entrepreneurs find that they can manage risk and reduce risk by doing a number of things, and we'll talk about three of those. We'll talk about their search for information, minimizing their investment, and maximizing their flexibility.

How does searching for information mitigate risk?

For the first element of searching for information, many entrepreneurs who are unsuccessful just start doing things. They fire before they aim. Instead, be planful. We still want to take action, but we want to think about what we're doing before we act.

As you explore ideas for new products, go into a retailer and see what's available, and think about what you may introduce that will still be competitive in six months. It may take you three months or six months to get your product to market, and many of the products that are in that retailer today are going to change over time. You have to think ahead—three months out, six months out, even years out—to what's going to be competitive then. You have to ask what new patents are being issued, and what new products are being demonstrated at trade shows. What new research is going to inspire new products?

Think about what's missing in the world and write that down, examine it, explore it, and begin to talk to other people about it.

The business model canvas is a risk management tool that we will discuss later. We'll also talk about business plan development, and while authoring a business plan doesn't guarantee your success, and while you may have many things wrong in the beginning, a key value of it is that it puts your thoughts and your ideas to paper. It forces you to connect disparate themes of thinking about what is my product, who is my customer, and what's my market? How am I going to finance it? What level of funding do I need? What team am I going to build? This aligns your ideas with your goals, a timeline for implementation, and quantitative measures to assess your progress. It puts you on path to doing research, analyzing markets, and understanding customers—and doing it all within a cohesive document. It's that search process, and that process of thinking, that is more valuable than the document itself.

How does minimizing your investment mitigate risk?

Customer discovery and customer validation are critical to product development and company building. Using lean startup principles, build a simple version of your product or service, a minimum viable product (MVP). Build a basic prototype, deploy it, and solicit feedback. A prototype in a very basic sense may be with paper, it may be with wood, it may be simply drawing what a website, an app, or a service may look like in a Word document or in PowerPoint. This is a very basic rendition before you're down the path of building something that's sellable.

Share this basic prototype with prospective customers to get their feedback before you invest the time and energy in building the real product. What would they change? What would they pay? Maybe you think you need five features, and maybe the customers only care about three. Maybe they're only willing to pay for two. Well, that lets you know not to spend the time or money to build that five feature product, because the customers don't want it and they're not willing to pay for it. You can discover which two features are important, and that's where you can focus your energy and your money.

Learn from this, refine the product, and build it again. In this way, you're able to move through multiple iterations of product development with real customer feedback. From an alpha, a beta, a version one, etc. The basic premise is to start with something simple. Get it to market as soon as possible. Get feedback, and then iterate.

How does maximizing flexibility mitigate risk?

The third element of risk reduction is maximizing flexibility. This lets you make those pivots and adaptations to your product or service at a lower cost. It lets you test different market segments and find out where you fit and how people are going to respond to what you're offering, and gives you the opportunity to adapt that or change that if needed. Simple ways to do this are trying to use off-the-shelf products rather than custom products. If you have a software concept, see if there is a white label solution out there. Use Squarespace or other tools to build the early versions of your product. This is a critical step in the customer validation process.

Startups should not start with websites, logos, and business cards. Start with validating the concept, thinking about the specific feature set, and testing that with customers to get their feedback.

In summary, entrepreneurs are not inherently risk-seekers. We simply seek risk differently than non-entrepreneurs, and make an effort to mitigate it and put that into practice. Have that idea. Build a version—a simple version. Try it. Test it. Measure feedback. Look at your data. Learn from your data. Build it a second time. Iterate through these cycles as fast as possible to get to something that's sellable. Search for information as you're working through these steps. Minimize your investment and maintain your flexibility along the way.

Are your interpersonal skills well developed?

In spite of popular opinion that entrepreneurship is a solo sport, it's a team activity. Entrepreneurs spend their time with co-founders, partners, and employees. There's time spent with customers and investors. There's time spent with the press. In all of these elements, strong *interpersonal skills* are an asset for entrepreneurs.

While interpersonal skills may be innate to select individuals, we can all improve our interpersonal skills through study and practice. Questions to consider as we assess our interpersonal skills may include:

- Do we isolate ourselves?
- Do we have difficulty expressing our feelings?
- Do we feel that others take advantage of us?
- Do we try and guess how we should act within a group?
- Do we take relationships seriously?
- Do we have problems developing intimate relationships?
- Do we ever feel guilty?

Based on a recent survey, there is a great divide in the interpersonal skills of today's workplace, particularly with millennials. When we look at how millennials describe themselves, we see that nearly 70% feel their interpersonal skills to be well developed. When we look at how experienced co-workers describe millennials, we see an entirely different story with less than 30% of millennials described as having well developed interpersonal skills.

Without seeing all of the data and studying the survey, I am unable to attest to the accuracy of it. I can say that this is a good representation that shows how we see ourselves may not be how others see us. And that's not only true with interpersonal skills; it's true of all of the behaviors that we will examine.

How can we understand and improve our interpersonal skills?

When we define interpersonal skills, we're addressing the skills related to relationships between people. This includes building relationships with new people, as well as renewing, maintaining, and enhancing our existing relationships. This requires effective communication, assertiveness, conflict resolution, and anger management.

With communication skills, listening is very important. We all listen with a filter based on our assumptions and beliefs. This filter influences our perceptions, for better or for worse. We should respond thoughtfully, and not simply react. Most importantly, we need to focus on understanding what's being said and clarify, to make sure we understand what's being expressed.

To improve your assertiveness, be specific and ask for what you want. Be direct. Deliver the message to whom it's intended. Own that message. Do not be fearful of communicating your needs and wants.

From a conflict resolution standpoint, focus on the problem, the root problem, and not the individual. Be direct, specific, and timely, while being positive and acknowledging and validating others' concerns. Seek alternative solutions, discuss next steps, and follow up.

From an anger management perspective, be aware of what you're feeling and notice the signs of anger building. We need to understand what's really angering us and not displace anger. We may need to de-escalate and take a break. We want to examine our options and visualize how we may respond. Think multiple steps ahead. What may I do? What will be their response? What will I do next? How will they respond? What will I do next? You can also develop activities that help you cope with anger.

What are the benefits of strong interpersonal skills?

There are many benefits to these interpersonal skills. It certainly improves the quantity and the quality of the relationships and friendships that you can form. It also improves our ability to access entrepreneurial opportunities. If you are known and liked, your awareness of opportunities and your ability to act on them is dramatically higher.

Building and maintaining relationships is the key. Knowing key stakeholders opens doors. It opens access to information and resources. It gives you the opportunity to facilitate new relationships. You may be able to bypass the normal communication streams. If you have friends in different organizations whom you can contact, you don't need to call the front desk. You don't need to send an email to info@, and you don't need to cold call anyone. You can leverage your relationships for introductions to bridge these paths.

This is a timely point to mention Dale Carnegie, who over 70 years ago published *How to Win Friends and Influence People*, which addressed fundamental ideas that are still valuable today. What are the tools and techniques to become a friendlier person? What are the proven ways to win people to your way of thinking? His book provides a reminder of things we know, and things to do that we may not have considered.

In summary, we know that others' perceptions of us are a truer measure of our interpersonal skills, and a truer measure of many of our internal behaviors, than our self-view. To improve your interpersonal skills, think about communication, assertiveness, conflict resolution, and anger management. We also want to focus on building and maintaining relationships. I emphasize maintaining the most. It's easier to keep a relationship and to keep in touch with a friend or a contact than to make a new one. With today's online tools—LinkedIn, Facebook, etc.—it's very easy to stay connected. I encourage you to use those types of tools to stay connected to your networks, and connect to new networks.

Are you rich in social capital?

Are you rich? Not rich in the traditional monetary sense, but are you rich in *social capital*?

To explore capital, we understand financial capital—money. We understand manufactured capital—something that's built or made. There's human capital—individuals and their talents and capabilities. There's intellectual capital, which includes patents, trademarks, and copyrights.

For entrepreneurs, social capital is incredibly valuable. It gives you tremendous access and tremendous relationships that either can't be bought, or would be expensive to buy or attain over time.

I'd like you to do a brief activity. I'd like you to start by listing up to five individuals per group among three different groups.

First, list by name your most *trusted* friends. Next, do a new grouping, of five individuals, with whom you accomplish *work*. This would be in a professional context, your coworkers. If you're not presently working in that kind of a setting, it could be in an organization that you're volunteering with—a social organization, a religious organization, people with whom you frequently accomplish work. There may be names that overlap with the trusted group. Create a third list of up to five people with whom you regularly *socialize* with—your social circle.

When we begin to analyze these networks in this way, we can look at age, education, gender, ethnicity, experience, expertise, and a variety of other factors. How different are these individuals in your *trust, work,* and *social* lists?

What we find for entrepreneurs is that the diverse social capital improves their startup's success. If everyone with whom I work and collaborate and socialize is like me – 40 years old, male, white, works in education, and has an engineering background – even though I may know 1,000 people of that profile, it's arguably no better than knowing one person. There is incredible redundancy. There's minimal differences in experience, skills, relationships, and perspectives.

When we define social capital, we're addressing the resources available in and through your personal relationships. Social capital is not limited to one degree of separation; it's whom you know and whom they know. Social capital gives you the opportunity to make connections through subsequent connections. It can be very expansive, and it can be measured in its size as well as in its quality and diversity.

Why build it? People with rich social capital, people with large and diverse networks, are better informed. They're more creative, they're more efficient, and they're better problem solvers. You can save time, you can save money, you can collaborate, and work smarter, when you have relationships in place. When we examine examples of this, it's not uncommon that successful startups breed other successful startups.

With the early PayPal team, they've gone on to bigger and better things. Three former PayPal engineers started YouTube. The former CFO of PayPal funded YouTube's launch. A former PayPal executive founded Yelp, and a coworker from PayPal funded it. PayPal alumnus Reid Hoffman founded LinkedIn. A former PayPal coworker funded it.

There are many instances where individuals have success within a startup and create subsequent startups. They build relationships, they understand skill sets, they understand personalities, and their interpersonal relationships form. They can establish social capital and stay connected, and do new things with one another in a variety of different ways.

Raising capital through social capital is the most common way that people find funding. The U.S. Small Business Association reports that 75% of new businesses find and secure financing via their social networks. Whom they know often enables entrepreneurs to have the financial capital to start their ventures. For most startups, it's the social capital that leads to the financial capital.

There are a breadth of opportunities to build your social capital. You can attend meetups. You can volunteer. You can go to events and conferences. You can participate in professional associations. You can associate with alumni clubs of your universities. You can join degree programs of people that have common interests; of course I suggest the online Master of Technology Entrepreneurship Program at the University of Maryland.

You can also make new programs, and make new organizations. If there's not a group that's accessible to you, start one. There are probably other people in your area with similar interests who would benefit from connecting with one another.

A number of online networking tools are emerging to reconnect with old friends, and create new contacts. LinkedIn is a leading provider in this category.

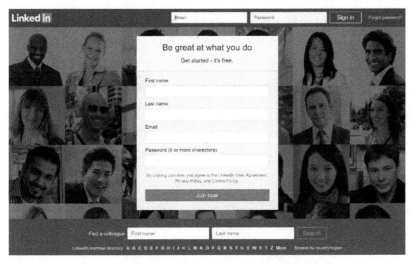

Figure 7. LinkedIn Website

In summary, recognize that social capital is exceptionally valuable to entrepreneurs. It's important to map and track and understand your network, and to keep the friends you have. It's easier to retain relationships, or renew relationships, than to form new ones. You should also be willing to go out and get involved. Get involved in organizations. Get involved in activities. Start your own organizations and activities. Work to build your social capital.

Entrepreneur Spotlight on Neil Blumenthal, Co-Founder and Co-CEO of Warby Parker

As director of a non-profit vision assistance program in El Salvador, Neil Blumenthal spent 5 years bringing glasses to people living on less than $4 per day. He soon realized that glasses can change lives, but only if they are attractive to wear. Neil recalls that "In the poorest village on the planet, people would rather be blind than wear a pair of used 1970s cat eyes."

This lesson in the desire for attractive eyewear at an affordable price was an influencer in Neil's creation of Warby Parker. In 2008, this New York City native enrolled in an MBA program, where he met his three future co-founders of the company. Their idea for Warby Parker was to build an online optical retailer that sold affordable, stylish glasses, and provide a pair to VisionSpring (the non-profit that Neil previously led) for every pair sold.

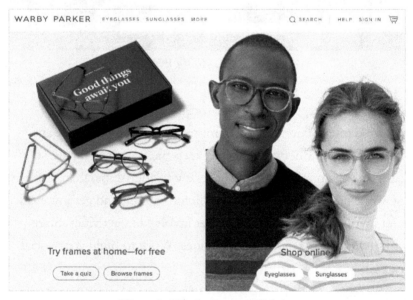

Figure 8. Warby Parker Website

In contrast to the existing companies in the eyewear market, Warby Parker integrated the design, development, production, and sales into their company. The efficiencies created by removing multiple companies in the middle (i.e. middlemen) brought costs savings to the end customer. The result is comparable-quality designer eyewear at half the price of many of their competitors. Warby Parker aims to deliver unique, vintage-inspired designs at a reasonable price while providing a pair to one in need with every pair sold.

Launched in early 2010, Warby Parker reached its first year's sales target within three weeks of starting the company. The company is now worth an estimated $1.75 billion.[10]

---

[10] Foster, T. (2018). "The Next Warby Parker. Inside the Wild Race to Overthrow Every Consumer Category". Inc. Magazine. www.inc.com

Ideas in Action: Entrepreneurial Behavior

With your awareness of the opportunities and challenges of strategic decision making, this activity challenges you to explore your entrepreneurial behavior as the third step of the Opportunity Analysis Canvas.

To facilitate your self-reflection, please discuss your entrepreneurial behavior by answering each of these questions. Your answers should be personalized based on your own experiences and perspectives.

How can you improve your confidence level and risk tolerance?	
What resources can you use to enhance your interpersonal relationship skills?	

How can you grow
your social capital?

Chapter 8: Part II – Seeing Entrepreneurially

Industry Condition

Industry Status

Macroeconomic Change

Competition

Successful entrepreneurs introduce a product or service that satisfies customer needs in a better way than competitors at a price that is greater than the cost of creating and delivering that product or service.

To understand how to fulfill customer needs at an attractive price, four areas are critical to assess: *industry condition, industry status, macroeconomic change,* and *competition.*

The Opportunity Analysis Canvas

Emphasis on "Part II – Seeing Entrepreneurially"

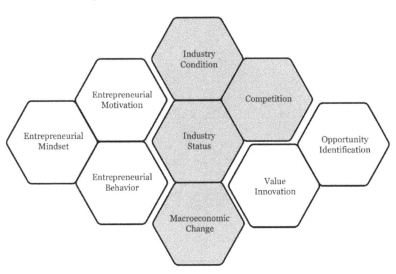

Chapter 9. Industry Condition

Our idea is to serve everybody, including people with little money.

Ingvar Kamprad

Founder of IKEA

After examining entrepreneurial mindset, motivation, and behavior, the next step in exploring entrepreneurial opportunities is evaluating *industry condition*. We can examine the rules of competition within an industry. This helps entrepreneurs to decide what industries they may want to enter, and which ones they may want to avoid. For those industries that they do choose to enter, entrepreneurs can better anticipate the opportunities and challenges therein.

Understanding the *knowledge conditions* and *demand conditions*, the two core segments of industry condition, provides insights into the attractiveness of an industry for new entrants. With this understanding, aspiring entrepreneurs can determine if, and how, to compete effectively within their chosen industry.

The Opportunity Analysis Canvas
Emphasis on "Industry Condition"

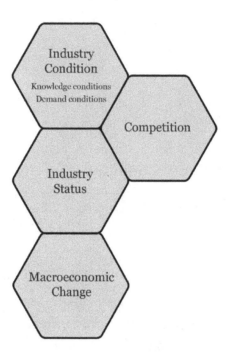

What impact do knowledge conditions have in your industry?

Knowledge conditions influence the success of entrepreneurs within their chosen industries. What we mean by knowledge conditions is the quantity as well as the quality of knowledge that is required to create and deliver the industry's products or services. Within a specific industry, what is the relative influence or importance of human expertise? What's the importance of knowledge within that industry? How does money, location, and relationships influence a company's success within that industry, as compared to knowledge?

Industries that are characterized by high knowledge conditions would be those that are intellectually difficult. They're fundamentally hard to enter and have a high barrier of entry. Industries that have low knowledge conditions would be those that perhaps anyone could enter if they had sufficient money, a viable location, or the right relationships.

By example, we can examine Squarespace once again. Anthony Casalena knew that, "I have a concept. I have a computer science degree, or at least am in a major to earn my degree, but I'm also teaching myself a lot of new things along the way. I'm teaching myself about marketing. I'm teaching myself about sales. I'm teaching myself about finance and accounting." As a one-person company, he was able to build the product and sell the product, and bring it to market, and generate income off of that version one. That gave him the opportunity to build a version two to generate more income. And that fueled the marketing for version three, which he built, brought to market, and so forth.

In its beginning, Squarespace was a blog building site. It had a fairly simple feature set, but it was still competitive versus its blog building competitors. It evolved into an expanded feature set. Anthony was always very effective at figuring out where the market was going, and what was important to his user base.

It's rare that one person can bring the technology skills and the business skills together to grow a company. It enabled him to eventually raise capital. He operated for approximately six years without any outside capital. He grew the product to over $1 million in revenue before he hired his first employee.

When he did eventually raise money in his sixth year of operations, he was able to retain majority ownership of his company due to his demonstrated success. He was able to retain over 60% ownership of his company even though he raised $38 million. He later raised another $40 million on path to an initial public offering (IPO).

When we think about where venture capitalists invest, the bulk of it is in high-tech, and industries that are very knowledge intensive. Software, biotech, media, entertainment, IT, industry, medical devices, consumer products—all are things that require deep expertise and are very knowledge-based. Money, location, and relationships alone do not result in success in high knowledge industries. Success is largely attributable to the founding team and the expanded team, and it takes a lot of knowledge to develop winning ideas into commercial successes.

How do you build knowledge within your startup?

By illustration, if you're a technologist, starting a tech company is a viable opportunity if you have the software skills, or the engineering skills, to build your product or service.

However, if you're interested in doing a tech startup and you're not a technologist, the path is much more challenging. Teaching yourself to write software or engineer products takes time. Your idea will also be difficult to secure funding for if you don't have the right team. The absence of a technologist on a tech team is a gap that investors have a hard time accepting.

If you're interested in starting a tech company, but lack the technical expertise, I strongly encourage you to seek a co-founder with the appropriate technical skills. Perhaps a colleague, or a former co-worker or classmate, is a fit.

There are even online communities to find co-founders. CoFoundersLab is one of the more popular ones, where if you have a concept, but you need to build a team, you can post your opportunity. You can keep the idea as vague as you wish, if you're concerned about sharing your idea with an unknown audience. Conversely, if you'd like to join a startup team, you can find people who are searching for people with your skill set. If you want to be an adviser, you can find opportunities to advise startups here as well.

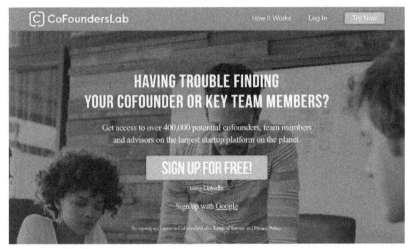

Figure 9. CoFoundersLab Website

If you don't have a technical co-founder, or need to supplement their technical skills, you can hire technical employees. You'll also likely hire later to build your startup's knowledge and expertise in finance, marketing, sales, and the other functions of the company.

You may also partner or joint venture to build the collective knowledge of your startup. A number of my students have created successful technology companies by partnership. They've had the vision. They've had the market insight. They've had the relationships in the industry. But they may not have had the programming talent, so they've been able to find other small companies that do product development and software development to partner with and form partnerships or joint ventures.

Outsourcing is a type of partnership that is typically short-term and project-based. For example, an entrepreneur may hire a small company or an individual that can do technical projects and tasks. Or it may be managed via an online community like Upwork. They offer an online network of individuals who are experts in various areas. You can post your project information there; they bid on that project. You select your winner, and you manage your project from there.

In summary, we need to understand the dynamics of the industries that we may enter, what it takes to succeed within different industries, and the rules of competition. As entrepreneurs, our best positioning is within industries with high levels of knowledge conditions. Consider how to leverage your knowledge, or acquire new knowledge. Knowledge can be learned. It can be realized via a co-founder. It can be employed. It can be outsourced. It can be partnered. There are a variety of ways that you can build that knowledge and expertise for your new venture.

What resources are best to research knowledge conditions?

While online searches via Google and other web browsers are a viable avenue to gathering insights on the knowledge conditions within an industry, the databases accessible via universities, libraries, etc. are particularly valuable. These databases provide reliable, comprehensive data and analysis on industries, competitors, and markets.

If you are a university student, or have access to a university library or community library, check to see if these databases are accessible for you:

- **Mergent Intellect:** Combines Hoover's Online, Key Business Ratios and D&B Million Dollar Database offering access to private and public U.S. and international business data, industry news, executive contact information, and industry profiles.

- **Business Source Complete:** Comprehensive database of business sources that includes over 3,600 peer reviewed journals, trade publications, magazines, books, case studies, company profiles, SWOT analyses, etc. To access Company Profiles, click on link from the "More" option menu top of screen (in the blue band) to search for Company profiles by Company name.

- **Factiva:** Provides full text access to over 8,000 business sources including national and international newspapers, magazines, wire services, web sites and Industry (trade) sources. Includes coverage of the Wall Street Journal.

- **Nexis Uni:** Covers business topics from local, regional and national newspapers, trade publications, business magazines, SEC filings, reference sources, key accounting sources, legal information as well as SWOT analyses. To find SWOT analysis information: (1) From 'Search by Content Type' (top right side of screen above search box), click on down arrow to select 'Company Profiles'; (2) click on 'Advanced Options'; (3) in the 'Build Your Own Segment' search box, enter the company of your choice and the type of publication in the following form (for example): 'Company(Microsoft) and Publication(SWOT)'; (4) click 'Apply'; (5) click 'Search'.

Are the demand conditions in your industry favorable?

As we explore the *demand conditions* within industries, we'll examine what these mean in the context of industry conditions and assess the influence of demand conditions on your success as an entrepreneur.

With demand conditions, we're addressing the size of the market, the rate of growth of that market, and the consistency of that market. To create a successful venture, we need to satisfy customer needs in a better way, and we need to do it in a profitable way.

A problem well stated is a problem half solved. We need to understand the customer's problems and to solve those known problems. We need to understand not only the current needs and wants in the market, but where the market's moving and how we're going to be competitive now and later. Critical to this understanding is customer discovery—that is, actually getting out of your building and examining prospective customers. What are the real customer needs and wants? Can these needs and wants be segmented into different types of customers? What is the relative importance of each individual need and want, and what are customers willing to pay for our solution?

For example, eLearning presents a complex set of demand conditions. As background:

- The global education expenditure is $4.4 trillion. There are 1.4 billion students, 62 million educators, and billions of parents who are influential in purchasing decisions.
- As a subset of the education market, eLearning is sizable as well, at $91 billion. It has a growth rate in the near term of 23% per year.
- For the "e" in eLearning, there are over 2.4 billion Internet users globally.

- The cost of higher education in the U.S. is up 84% since 2000.
- College students' loan debt in the U.S. exceeds $1 trillion, an all-time high.

Beyond the numbers, I need to understand the sentiment for eLearning. There is a lot of hype. There is a lot of expectation. There is a belief by many that eLearning is going to be a cure-all for education. I need to be aware of these sentiments. I need to be aware of these trends and desires and expectations, the hype and the facts.

There are new federal and regional regulations emerging in the eLearning space that I need to understand if I'm considering starting a new venture in this area.

There's also the rapid rise of massive open online courses (MOOCs), of open education, and free content.

When we consider eLearning and the demand in the marketplace, we see there's a variety of conditions to examine regarding the magnitude of the market, the rate of growth, the homogeneity of it, as well as the other factors that are influencing demand. Affordability of education, web access, computer and tablet ownership, and industry standards all play a role. The expenses incurred by the various types of education and technology suppliers is an important element to consider as well. Of course, I need to know who my customers are and who's influencing their buying decision.

My entrepreneurial opportunity analysis may include considering one of four education markets to enter with my new venture: K-12, undergraduate college students, graduate college students, or corporate and government employee training.

Through my research, I know that 50% of total education spending in the U.S. is done in the K-12 market. Not surprising, based on that being the bulk of the population. There are many more schools, and many more students, in K-12 than there are in colleges.

I need to recognize how the education industry is structured and how is it segmented.

Content is an area that's influenced by regulatory and curriculum matters, and the types of businesses that would fall into this category are the content publishers – curriculum designers within schools, textbook publishers, etc.

There are also management systems – software platforms, the tools, the smart technologies, the learning management systems, the analytics, etc. – that are part of the education and eLearning systems.

A third element is distribution. Arguably the most popular of late, this includes online access to courses and resources, free or paid. Types of businesses include immersive learning that strives to make face-to-face learning, or hybrid learning more experiential and more customized. It's MOOCs. It's other learning portals.

All three of these elements – content publishers, management systems, and distribution – will play a role in serving customers.

As I explore demand, I am curious of my prospective competitors in the market and their success in raising investment capital. Are companies getting funding from venture capitalists and other types of investors? With research, I see that they are, even though it's on a modest decline. It rose steadily into 2010, but with the U.S. and the global economic slowdown, investment began to level off in eLearning startups. It's not surprising, recognizing that many of the K-12 and college institutions are publicly funded, meaning they're reliant on tax revenues and government spending. If government spending declines, there's often a negative impact on the companies reliant on schools and colleges as customers. In 2014, there were approximately 100 eLearning companies funded by venture capitalists.

We also need to understand the merger and acquisition activity in the space, and what's going on there. There is a lot of consolidation via acquisitions, with the total values of these deals approaching $10 billion. eLearning companies accounted for 75% of the education companies that were merged or acquired.

We can also see who's raising money, from whom, in what target sector, and at what transaction value. We see notable investors that include venture capitalists like Andreessen Horowitz, as well as foundations, like the Bill and Melinda Gates Foundation, placing money into eLearning. With research, we can see the target sectors and we can see transaction values—a few million dollars here, $10 or $15 million there.

When we examine demand conditions, there are variety of databases that we have access to, both free and paid. There are many research databases, such as BizStats, the U.S. Census Bureau, and SBDCs in the U.S., and Eurostat in the European Union.

To capitalize on these demand conditions, the magnitude of the demand is important. But when you're exploring an early stage industry, the magnitude may not necessarily be high today. We're more interested in the rate of growth of future demand. If it's a small market today, that's okay; but if it's growing at 20%, or 30%, or 40% a year, we want to be on that curve as entrepreneurs. We want to ride that growth. The idea is that a rising tide will raise many of the companies that are in that space.

We're also interested in the consistency of demand across the customer segments. For our eLearning example, I see that half of the market spend is K through 12, which is a fairly homogeneous market. There are probably a similar set of needs and wants across that broad segment. Now, that doesn't mean that I necessarily want to try and build a product that's going to serve everyone. The needs of a kindergarten class and the needs of a high school class are very different. The sophistication of the students is very different. What a six-year-old and an eighteen-year-old can do is very different. It's not all the same or a one-size-fits-all situation, but at least it brings me into a common category of needs and wants. There's a grading system, and assignments and homework that's common. There's a teacher-student relationship, and a parent or guardian relationship to the schools. The administrators in the K through 12 area will play a role, and there may be various regulations regarding student privacy that are common.

If we're interested in corporate training, or the training of employees within the government, by the government, it's a different set of factors and concerns. That's what we mean by consistency of demand or the pockets of demand where there's a large grouping of K through 12, a large grouping of the post-secondary, a large grouping of corporate and government, where if we were to develop a solution we could tackle one of those large areas with our solution and not have to build an entirely new solution if we wanted to compete within that area.

This raises the question of once you've recognized an industry and began to dissect the demand, what do you do from there? For me, I ask where is there an unrealized opportunity.

If everyone that I'm seeing, particularly those who are raising venture capital, are in the distribution part of eLearning, then I, as a startup, may not want to compete there. I do not want to chase what everyone else is chasing. I want to do something different. In distribution, there are a lot of players and a lot of funding.

On the content side, perhaps I can be a content generator. My expectancy, however, is that the colleges and the schools may already have the content, or may have the expertise to develop that content, or even the responsibility, philosophically, to develop their own content.

I may want to start a company in the management system part of eLearning, and focus on new management tools that can be of value. Maybe I don't want to compete as a provider of all tools; perhaps I can specialize in only mobile tools – tablets, smartphones, etc. And I may not want to develop all of the mobile tools; I could start with analytics, within mobile, as a part of the management system.

This is the scope of demand-side thinking that you can do to determine where you want to compete. Think about where the opportunity lies. Where is there sufficient magnitude, an attractive rate of growth, and relative homogeneity where you can build a sustainable startup? Can you identify a sizeable market that is growing, that has similar needs and wants, to which you can deliver something of value? And can you do it in an area where perhaps there's a niche that for you is attractive. You may find that there are opportunities to pursue, opportunities that are too small to attract large companies, but very worthwhile for you as a startup. For me, a $1 million opportunity would be very attractive. At Microsoft or Google, they wouldn't answer the phone for a $1 million opportunity. They wouldn't take a meeting to discuss a $1 million opportunity. It would be too small for companies at that scale.

When you're thinking about demand, segmentation is a central piece to consider as well. Segmentation provides an opportunity to specialize and to build your reputation and brand for doing one thing well, which you can leverage into new things later. It gives you discipline, and allows you to focus on specific needs and wants of a specific customer.

In summary, when we consider demand conditions, recognize this as a critical piece of the industry that we need to understand. As we look to bring new products to market, we want to recognize the influence that magnitude, rate of growth, and homogeneity play in our venture's success.

What resources are best to research demand conditions?

While online searches via Google and other web browsers are also a viable avenue to gathering insights on the demand conditions within an industry, the databases accessible via universities, libraries, etc. are particularly valuable in this instance as well.

If you are a university student, or have access to a university library or community library, check to see if these databases are accessible for you:

- IBIS World:
    - Click "US Industry Reports" to browse reports by industry sectors.
    - Or, in the search field for "Search by keyword, company or code", you may start with a keyword search.
- D&B Hoovers:
    - Click on the "Research Industries" button and search for your desired industry.
    - Or, in the search field for "Search Industries by Name or Code", click on "Browse" to see the options or enter a keyword to begin your search.

Entrepreneur Spotlight on Jeff Raider,
Co-Founder and Co-CEO of Harry's

When exploring high-demand opportunities, the shaving razor and blade is among the most popular product categories worldwide. The knowledge needed to design and engineer a new, competitive product in this very established market is a challenge, as is the know-how to brand, market, and distribute the product successfully.

Jeff Raider shares that the idea for Harry's started when a friend complained of poor customer service and a high bill when buying razor blades and shaving cream at a drugstore. That friend, Andy Katz-Mayfield, became his co-founder and co-CEO at their shaving company, Harry's, which they launched in February 2013.

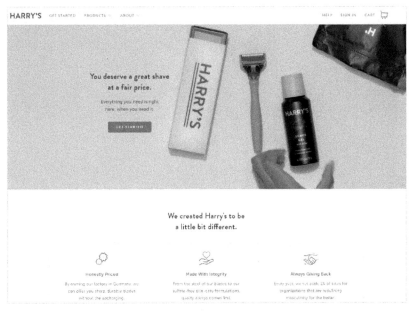

Figure 10. Harry's Website

They have focused on designing ergonomic, aesthetically pleasing, and durable razor handles and blades. They also developed a moisturizer-laden shaving cream.

When asked about the competition, Jeff responds, "It's a big market, it's dominated by a couple of companies, they make huge products and they charge lots and lots of money for products that are difficult to make." Jeff believes that Harry's can make and sell better products for less money than the competition.[11]

Their strategy includes direct selling to customers via their online store. "We felt like we had to take a new approach in established markets to build our differentiated brands," says Jeff. "Big name brands at times don't communicate directly with customers, and we've found customers like brands that care about them and exist to try to deliver a great experience."[10]

---

[11] Ryssdal, K. (2013). "After Warby Parker, a clean shave with Harry's." Marketplace. Available at http://www.marketplace.org/topics/business/corner-office/after-warby-parker-clean-shave-harrys.

Ideas in Action: Industry Condition

With new insights on how entrepreneurs decide what industries they may want to enter, and which ones they may want to avoid, you can better anticipate the opportunities and challenges therein.

This activity challenges you to explore industry conditions as the fourth step of the Opportunity Analysis Canvas. Your answers should be personalized based on your own interests and ambitions.

What knowledge do you possess that can contribute to serving a market need?	
What are the demand conditions in the market?	

Chapter 10. Industry Status

If General Motors had kept up with technology like the computer industry
has, we would all be driving $25 cars that got 1,000 miles per gallon.

Bill Gates

Co-founder of Microsoft

With industry conditions addressing the knowledge and
demand factors, it's important to understand *industry lifecycle* and
industry structure as the key components of *industry status*. By
studying industry status, aspiring entrepreneurs can assess an
industry's timeliness for new entrepreneurial entrants.

We'll discuss how industries evolve, and what happens as new
competitors emerge. I'll also help you recognize the timelines and
windows of opportunity that are going to maximize your success
within an industry.

The Opportunity Analysis Canvas
Emphasis on "Industry Status"

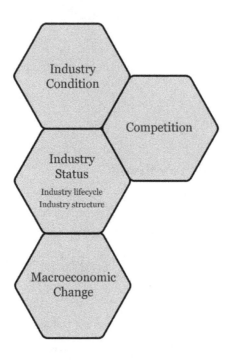

What is the lifecycle stage of your industry?

With *industry lifecycle*, we're addressing the life of the industry. What's the lifecycle of a person? What are the normal stages of a person? You can go all the way back to conception, then there's a baby, and a child. There's young adult and adult, middle age, old age, and death. Businesses often live on a similar cycle. They're conceived, they grow, and they mature. Eventually, most businesses will die.

Every year *Fortune* magazine ranks the top 500 companies based on revenues in the U.S. How many companies from the 1930 *Fortune 500* – the 500 biggest companies in the U.S. – are still on the list today? 400? 200? It's actually fewer than 50.

What happened to the other 450? Well, their assets were

taken over and developed into something else by other companies. There were businesses that died. Wagon wheel companies died, horse-and-buggy companies died, and in their places other companies emerged.

Focus on being an early entrant into an industry to maximize your chances for success. If the year is 1990, you don't want to start manufacturing rotary phones. You want to start manufacturing mobile phones.

Where can you be an early entrant? You will find that it's far easier to attract customers when there aren't existing market leaders in the space. For example, if you're interested in buying a new smartphone, you're probably going to look to Apple or Samsung. Perhaps Motorola or the Google Pixel. Your options are relatively slim. Probably not a market that you'd want to enter today as a startup. There a few companies in the market, and these few companies do it very well. They have the brand, the relationship. There are technical standards that have emerged.

As an emerging industry, consider eBooks. eBook sales are projected to pass print book sales soon, according to PricewaterhouseCoopers. Why?

Will young students begin receiving textbooks provided by their school in eBook form instead of print? If K-12 schools purchased eBooks and tablets instead of printed textbooks, this alone would dramatically increase the eBooks market.

Will new features enabled by eBooks versus print books create a new eBook following among readers? You should be able to do things with an eBook that you can't do with a print book. You should be able to tap on a word and see a definition, picture, or video.

What's it mean when you have a product that has more features than the preceding product? What should that mean about the price point? It should be higher, right? I have a product that's better. It's portable. It's more durable. It's environmentally friendly. It has new features and functions. Click, and I can save and highlight and share. I can purchase it immediately, without the drive to a bookstore or waiting on a delivery. I can do all these things with an eBook that I can't do with a print book. However, many people still balk at being charged more for an eBook than a print book.

Why would people be against paying more for an eBook? There's that physical aspect. There's that tactile sensation of a print book to which we're accustom. This is part of consumer behavior. The customer's willingness to pay is still evolving.

Interestingly, while eBook sales are increasing dramatically, dedicated eBook devices are decreasing dramatically. Now that's not intuitive. You would think that if eBook sales were increasing, it would mean that people are going to need to buy eBook readers for the first time. However, iPads and tablets are replacing dedicated eBook readers.

Kindle, as it was initially conceived as an eBook reader, is winding down. Now they have the Kindle Fire, which is more tablet-like, with broad features and functions.

What's the market opportunity for you? Should you enter the eBook device market? Probably not. Should you enter the tablet market? Probably not. Why not? Because that core technology's already there. It's too late. You're already behind the curve. And you probably don't want to compete against Apple, Amazon, and Samsung.

Is there an opportunity for you in the eBook area anyway? How can you compete or participate in this market if you're not going to start an eBook reader or a tablet company?

There are many ways to participate in the growing eBook

market. You could build apps. You could build accessories. What do people buy after they purchase a tablet? They buy a case. They want screen protectors or external speakers. Consider a company called ZeroChroma, started by an engineering graduate from the University of Maryland. They recognized and acted on an opportunity in this space to do a new style of iPhone and iPad cases.

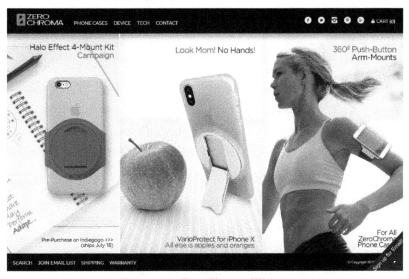

Figure 11. ZeroChroma Website

Recognize that young industries favor new firms, and there's substantially less competition versus established industries. There's more of a level playing field. If you're not out there trying to compete with Apple, you're trying to compete with the two or three companies that are making software that's trying to convert docs to mobi files for eBooks, for example. That's a more feasible space to enter. The big brands are not there yet. Their relationships are not there yet. These small competitors may have more money than you, but they don't have an Apple level of money.

In summary, when we think about industry lifecycle, I emphasize that new ventures tend to perform better in younger industries. They have the opportunity to enter a market that is relatively immature. There's less competition and more of a level playing field to enter as a new venture with other smaller firms. Startups can effectively compete for customer loyalties. If the industry is new, if there are not major competitors already in play, and if there are not already major brands in play, startups have an easier time attracting customers.

What is the structure of your industry?

To understand *industry structure*, we examine the barriers to entering the industry and the competitive dynamics within the industry. The key factors to assess within industry structure are: *capital intensity, advertising intensity, company concentration,* and *average company size.*

Is the industry capital intensive?

Capital intensity is the amount of money required to enter and compete within an industry. Industries that have a high capital intensity are things like automotive manufacturing. Industries that have a low capital intensity would be something like a website that you start to provide movie reviews, where, for perhaps $10, you can launch a website driven by a website builder. If you can use Microsoft Word, you can build a site using one of these website builders. You can watch movies. You can post your reviews of those movies. It's very easy and inexpensive to start.

Online tutoring is an industry that I see a lot of interest in among students. There's strong growth due to rising Internet adoption for educational purposes, and there's a large number of individuals enrolled in educational institutions. There is growth in the industry of 7.9% annually. We also see that there's growth in competition, and that's anticipated to increase annually at 5.8% to 208 competitors. Online tutoring services reported revenues of $146.9 million this year, with profits of $12.3 million.

While this broad data is readily accessible via research reports from IBIS and others, our job as entrepreneurs is to perform further research and analysis. Based on the above data, I can perform further calculations. I can divide the revenues, expenses, profits, etc. by the 208 companies to see the average values per company. I can also study the industry leaders to learn their strategies and struggles.

Tutor.com owns 15.9% of the market, and if I multiply that 15.9% by the $146.9 million total industry revenues, I know what their revenues were for the year. I can do the same math with Pearson PLC.

I can also examine the product and service segmentation. I see that 56% of the revenues generated were from exam preparation services. That 28% were focused on other tutoring programs, probably one-to-one tutoring.

Competition is very high, which is often the case when you're dealing with low-capital-intensity businesses like tutoring. If it's easy for you to enter, it's likely easy for others.

There's rapid technology and process change. There's growing customer acceptance of online tutoring. And there's rapid introduction of new products and new brands. All good signs for me, as an entrepreneur, that we are indeed in a growth phase.

When I look at capital intensity, I want to see where money is being spent. I see that it is predominantly spent on labor.

Beyond the tutors, the other half of online tutoring is the technology. The report tells me that technology is majority bought and not built, and that's an important differentiation for startups. Bought means paying for a service, in this case perhaps Adobe Connect, WebEx, or other tools that can be used to support online tutoring. They may integrate screen sharing, video conference capability, or other areas, whereby the tutors and the students can have quality interaction.

In large part, these companies are not building their own technology platforms. They're able to leverage tools or services that are already out there, either in whole or in part, and adapt them to their needs. Now that's not necessarily true of all companies. They may build their own solution. Or they use off-the-shelf solutions to serve their initial needs, and once they realize success and profit, they can afford to have a custom solution built for them.

On average, across the 208 companies, they're at a relative low level of capital intensity. It's more labor-intensive than it is capital-intensive. And even for that labor, the expense may not be very high. There's a measure of expertise that they need, but it may not necessarily be a Ph.D. level of expertise. It may not require $100,000-a-year employees.

How can low-capital opportunities be identified?

Every year *Entrepreneur Magazine* ranks the top ten low-cost franchises for the year. Low-cost for them can be a few thousand dollars. So for $2,000, or $3,000, or $4,000, you can be a franchise owner. And the franchises vary. There are a lot of cleaning services, tax preparation services, and exercise services. There are a number of travel planning services.

JAN-PRO is a commercial cleaning service with over 11,000

locations in the U.S. and abroad. Twenty-five years ago it started as many franchises do, with an entrepreneur with a concept who launches a company and has success. He's then able to sell that model and that brand to others who want to implement it. The costs of doing that are a franchise fee and a royalty, which is a percentage of revenues. What we see for JAN-PRO is a very low cost of entry: $1,000 in cash, and a total investment starting at $3,100, with the option of financing the equipment. If you need a van and cleaning equipment, which you would as a new entrant, JAN-PRO will facilitate the financing. There is very low capital intensity. My expectation is that the profits are rather low as well.

How can aspiring entrepreneurs, particularly those with a more innovative ambition, participate in commercial cleaning differently than joining JAN-PRO?

You could start a commercial cleaning company, but it may not necessarily be the lifestyle, or generate the profits, that you may envision.

You could start a technology company with an online training platform that supports new commercial cleaners. If you see an opportunity in that space and you're exploring another low-capital way of participating, for JAN-PRO and the other commercial services companies that are starting, you can provide supplementary training. Perhaps it's training on how to physically do the work. Or your platform could support the marketing and business operations of these commercial cleaners. They could use your online training platform to develop the skills and the know-how to be successful in that marketplace. Or perhaps it's something else.

In summary, when we look at industry structure, we want to think about the role that it plays within the industries that we're considering entering, and how best to compete. We also want to recognize that low capital intensity presents a more affordable opportunity for new entrants to enter and compete effectively. There may be a race to outpace and out-innovate others in the space. If you're an early entrant, can you create entry barriers – with your brand, with your distribution, with exclusivity agreements, etc. – to make it more expensive for future competitors? The key element is to recognize the role of capital intensity and the influence that it has on the industry structure.

Is the industry advertising intensive?

When we consider *advertising intensity*, we're exploring the importance of advertising and branding to the success of competitors in a specific industry.

Industries with high advertising intensity are characterized by customers who prefer to buy based on past successful transactions, brands they know, or products about which they've heard. Established companies that have a reputation for success are going to have a unique advantage in high advertising intensity industries, and new ventures have a harder time competing.

There may also be perks in play, things like loyalty programs that are offered by credit card companies, airlines, hotels, and retailers that make it more difficult for new entrants to compete. Now for many of us we may not be starting a credit card company, hotel, or airline, but we want to recognize that increasingly there are other technology-based firms and small firms that are doing similar things. They're building and populating profiles, integrating networks, and building up preference engines. They are developing one-click transactions online, and doing other things that add more stickiness or adherence to their customers on those selected platforms and sites. We want to think broadly about the variety of things that can take place, and that can influence advertising, and influence the resistance of a customer to trying something new.

When we look at industries with low advertising intensity, customers here are more willing to try new products and to try new brands. There may be other influences in play—there may not be established product leaders or established brands in that space. There may be low switching costs, so it's easy for consumers to experiment and try a variety of different things before committing to one thing. There may be differentiation and/or another value that the new products deliver. The preferred scenario for new ventures is to be able to operate inside lower advertising intensity industries.

Let's continue our example of online tutoring and think about the advertising element. While instructional techniques may vary tutor to tutor, the same general purpose of educating students remains. As a result, new firms must be willing to spend large sums of money on advertising. That's not good news if you're a new entrant in the online tutoring space. What is large? How do you quantify large? Well, it could be a percent of revenue. The average company will spend 1.6% of their revenues on marketing. For online tutoring it's more than twice that: 3.8% of revenues are spent on marketing. And if you're an unknown firm with an unknown brand, a new entrant, you're likely going to have to spend a lot more than that—maybe 10%, maybe 20%. That essentially would make your profit go to zero, and perhaps be zero for a year or two as you build your brand and market awareness.

We also want to think about who's our customer. In the online tutoring space, perhaps our customers are public schools or private schools. Perhaps they are public universities, or private universities, or for profit universities. It's the student themselves, or the parents, to whom we're going to try and sell our product and market to, or maybe a combination. There are options for those we want to target, and the expense of targeting them is something we want to consider as well. The relative influence of advertising on their decision of what to buy and what not to buy should be part of our decision of our target market.

Once we've identified them, we can do fairly simple things. We can look at mailing lists that are out there. If we want to target the schools or the universities, we could spend all day and all night on websites trying to collect contact information for people at universities that we think would be interested, or we could buy lists. We could buy contact lists of names and phone numbers or emails of influencers at these different schools and universities, and that may be a more effective way of spending our time and money. Or, if we're trying to sell directly to consumers, and we're trying to find households of a certain income level and a certain geography that have school-aged children, whatever our profile is, our demographic and our behavior profiles, we may be able to find those on a purchased list.

Perhaps social media is the answer, and we'll become a viral marketing sensation. Well, good luck with that. This is a complex challenge that requires thoughtful planning and sound execution.

We can develop a profile of the various tools and techniques, as well as companies and providers in the online marketing space. This does not include anything you may do via print. It does not include anything that you may do via other media and channels. It does not include conferences where you may exhibit.

Advertising is a complicated puzzle driven by the core values you're delivering, the audiences that you're targeting, and the relative advertising intensity that you're up against.

In summary, by studying industry structure, aspiring entrepreneurs can assess the industry's timeliness for new entrepreneurial entrants, and better understand how to compete. Low advertising intensity industries present a more affordable opportunity for new entrants to enter and compete effectively. This also suggests that the brand loyalty of incumbents is more surmountable by new entrants.

Are you trying to enter a concentrated market?

Market concentration can present an opportunity or a challenge for us in entrepreneurship. When we look at this and we think about what's the ideal, we would like a small number of small-sized competitors.

For online tutoring, we identified 208 competitors. Four competitors generate 23.6% of total revenues in the market. The remaining 204 share 78.4% of the market.

The market leader, with 15.9%, is Tutor.com. Founded in 1998, they started within a couple of years of the mainstreaming of the Internet. Their annual revenues of $23.4 million, and their average profit margin of 7%, are impressive.

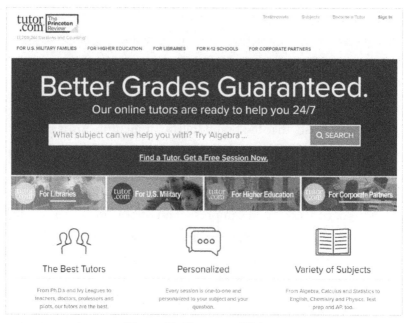

Figure 12. Tutor.com Website

The next largest competitor is Pearson PLC, at $8.4 million in annual revenues. They're in 200 schools and they have 100,000 students. Pearson PLC's online tutoring businesses are TutorVista and Smarthinking.

We can also think about concentration based on geography. Now, as an online business, one could argue you could be based anywhere, nationally, or internationally. But what we may find is that there are certain advantages to being near customers, or near partners, or near investors. That's what we're seeing here. We're seeing a higher concentration of these online tutoring businesses in California and in New York. There are a lot of schools, there are a lot of students, and there are a lot of prospective funders and investors. So, that's something to think about, as well— where you want to locate. Not only what's feasible, because for an online business, arguably, anywhere is feasible. Ask where you can be near customers, where you can be near prospective partners, where you can be near investors, and where you can be appropriately near your employee base. In the education sector, it's also a question of what state or locality you are targeting because of applicable state and local education standards and regulations.

In summary, when we think about market concentration, we'd like a small number of competitors, and preferably small competitors. It's not always the reality of our industry. But, it is important to recognize, and it helps guide the strategies that we're developing. It helps us create and market better products.

It also lets us think about the opportunity for partnering. We see this at times in the airline industry and financial services, where our number three and number four competitors may team up and merge, and try to compete more effectively with the number one and number two. You may informally have collaborations and other partnerships, perhaps with competitors, or near competitors. This may be something that you want to consider longer term, regarding opportunities to either formally joint venture, or merge.

If you are competing in a space where there are a high number of competitors, another thing you can think about is where's your niche? Can you develop a better way, a different way? Can you target a different profile of customer? Can your business model be sharply focused? Within online tutoring, can you specialize on certain age groups, or certain subjects, or target certain price points, or specialize in languages? Try and differentiate yourself from what's out there, which is a good idea anytime, but is particularly valuable when you're facing high-market concentration.

What is the average size of a company in the industry?

The *average size* of your competitors is an important issue to examine. We're going to look at that in the context of industry status and its impact on starting the venture. This is within our element of industry structure of the Opportunity Analysis Canvas, and it's defined by the resources of competitors. It's the number of employees and other capital and resources that these competitors have on average.

When we examine startups, we see that many are one or two people. We see that 85% of them are supporting the startup almost exclusively from their own savings, or from other consulting work that they're doing on the side.

When we look at their startup problems, more than 50% are facing product development problems, particularly for technology-based products.

Nearly 30% are struggling with time issues. This is influenced by their funding strategies. If they're doing consulting and side projects to fund their primary objective of the startup, naturally that's taking time away from the primary goal.

Approximately 20% are struggling with their marketing and sales efforts.

Based on this data, it's valuable to have a technology background, technology experience, or technologists on your team if you're doing a tech venture. But if it's not a well formed team, or if it's a very small team, you may be without the sales and marketing expertise. A variety of different challenges are faced based on the experience, expertise, and funding of startups.

When we think about an ideal competitor size, we would like to have small competitors in our space—companies that are more comparably resourced to what we are as startups.

In online tutoring, the sizes of competitors are widely varied.

Industry leader Tutor.com was acquired in January of 2012, by IAC/InterActiveGroup, a $3 billion revenue-generating company that owns about.com, ask.com, dictionary.com, College Humor, OK Cupid, the Daily Beast, Vimeo, Tinder, and others. Tutor.com is a well-resourced company based on their parent company.

The TutorVista and Smarthinking brands are similarly positioned with their ownership company, Pearson PLC. Pearson PLC is a multi-national conglomerate with over 40,000 employees.

We can further examine our 208 competitors and the $147 million in revenue generated last year. We can divide these revenues by the number of competitors to calculate the average revenue per competitor. We can perform a similar calculation to learn that the average number of employees per competitor is 25. While the two largest competitors are rather large, the vast majority of the 208 competitors are rather small at 25 employees.

We examine key financial ratios, and consider revenues and expenses per employee. In 2014, we see $30,000 revenue per employee on average against $13,000 average annual wages. This $13,000 would suggest that, on average, these companies are paying a minimum wage, or we may find that there are a lot of part-time employees. This gives us insights into the industry and how the economics of it are structured.

In summary, when we examine industry status, we find that new ventures perform better in younger industries with immature industry structures. We find there's less competition than if you're trying to compete within established industries. We find that capital intensity and advertising intensity tend to be lower in younger industries. It's more affordable for new entrants to be competitive. We also want to recognize that young industries offer a common learning curve and comparable branding opportunities among competitors. This presents entrepreneurs with a more level playing field, and improves their likelihood of success.

What resources are best to research the industry status?

While online searches via Google and other web browsers are also a viable avenue to gathering insights on the industry status, the databases accessible via universities, libraries, etc. are particularly valuable in this instance as well.

If you are a university student, or have access to a university library or community library, check to see if these databases are accessible for you:

- IBIS World:
    - Click "US Industry Reports" to browse reports by industry sectors.
    - Or, in the search field for "Search by keyword, company or code", you may start with a keyword search.
- D&B Hoovers:
    - Click on the "Research Industries" button and search for your desired industry.
    - Or, in the search field for "Search Industries by Name or Code", click on "Browse" to see the options or enter a keyword to begin your search.

Entrepreneur Spotlight on Joel Jackson, Founder and CEO of Mobius Motors

Joel Jackson's vision for Mobius Motors started in 2009 when he was working with a startup forestry venture in rural Kenya. He spent time with local farming communities and lived many of their day-to-day challenges, including a lack of mobility. Many people would walk tens of miles to school, to the physician, or to find clean drinking water. This birthed the idea for a new automotive manufacturing company designed and built in Africa for its people. While the automotive industry is highly developed and mature in the more affluent regions of the world, it is in its infancy in Africa.

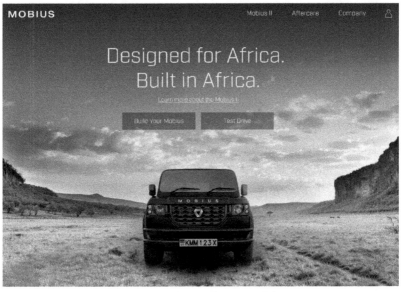

Figure 12. Mobius Motors Website

Mobius aimed to build a more appropriate and affordable ($6,000-$10,000) vehicle for transport businesses and create a platform for mobility across Africa. Production costs and weight are drastically reduced by removing non-essentials like power steering, air conditioning, and glass windows. Investments are increased in areas of critical functionality such as rugged suspensions and durability on highly degraded roads.[12]

Mobius vehicles are manufactured in a purpose-built production facility in Nairobi. The Mobius production team builds each vehicle, from the body shop area where the space-frame is manufactured, to the paint shop, and then onto general assembly and final line inspections. Mobius utilizes internationally recognized quality controls throughout the production line to build each vehicle to world-class lean manufacturing standards.

By 2013, Mobius had 24 employees. They built two prototype vehicles and one production alpha vehicle. The initial proof-of-concept production of 50 vehicles rolled out in 2013. Mobius raised several million dollars of investment and increased production to 300 vehicles in 2014.[13]

In time, Joel Jackson believes that the mass production of Mobius vehicles will enable systemic change in Africa's transit network. He hopes to contribute to a prosperous future for hundreds of millions of people across the continent.

---

[12] Mobius Motors (2013). Corporate website. http://www.mobiusmotors.com

[13] Peabody, J. (2013). Q&A with Joel Jackson, founder of Mobius Motors. Reuters blog on small business. Available at http://blogs.reuters.com/small-business/2013/05/23/q-a-with-joel-jackson-founder-of-mobius-motors/

Ideas in Action: Industry Status

With new insights on how entrepreneurs decide what industries they may want to enter, and which ones they may want to avoid, you can better anticipate the opportunities and challenges therein.

This activity challenges you to explore industry status as the fifth step of the Opportunity Analysis Canvas. Your answers should be personalized based on your own interests and ambitions.

What is the lifecycle stage of the industry that you are interested in entering?	
What is the capital intensity within your chosen industry?	

What is the advertising intensity within your chosen industry?	
What is the company concentration within your chosen industry?	
What is the average company size within your chosen industry?	

Chapter 11. Macroeconomic Change

Luck is what happens when preparation meets opportunity.

Seneca

Roman philosopher

Macroeconomics deals with the performance of a large economy and its vast number of influencing factors. For entrepreneurs, it's valuable to understand how the needs and wants of your target audience are influenced by the world around them.

This chapter explores this complex world, with an emphasis on *demographic* and *psychographic* changes. Changes in *technology, society, politics,* and *regulations* are also examined, as these are central to entrepreneurs' understanding of their customers' buying behaviors.

The Opportunity Analysis Canvas
Emphasis on "Macroeconomic Change"

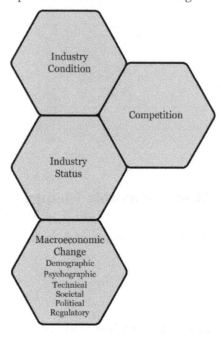

What demographic changes are creating new market opportunities?

Demographic changes can present a host of opportunities for new ventures. Our definition of demographic changes is simply the observable characteristics of populations. It provides insights into where opportunities exist within markets. It also gives us insights on how to develop appropriate business and marketing strategies to target those customers.

We may be able to gain insights on the demographics of our target customers by examining research on our competition. For example, a recent report examined Pinterest, a popular online platform for sharing photos. Within the Pinterest user base, the annual household income is over $100,000, 50% of its users have children, and 68% are female. By age, the highest concentration is between 25 and 34, with a secondary concentration between 35 and 44.

If we were creating a competitor to Pinterest, this type of data would assist us in understanding our customer, how to serve them effectively, and how to market to them.

There are many demographic changes going on within the U.S.: an aging population, increasing ethnic diversity, and a society challenged by obesity. All are opportunities for entrepreneurs. There are opportunities in developing assisted living centers. There are opportunities in foreign language media. There are opportunities in weight control tools, as we've seen with the rise of fitness and diet-related apps and gadgets.

Entrepreneurs should know the income and purchasing power of their target customers, as well as their age, family status, residential status, gender, and education. These are all things that are important to know and understand as you are either exploring opportunities, or trying to understand the audiences that you'll serve.

There are a number of databases with demographics data. American FactFinder and the State and County Quick Facts are U.S.-based resources. There are comparable resources in other regions of the world. These are often developed by the government and/or organizations.

For example, with American FactFinder I can examine Bethesda, Maryland. I can examine the population density. I can examine age, race, households, housing tenure and a variety of different factors, as well as the percentage distribution of those factors across these populations. I can do this for every sizeable city in the U.S.

I can explore education, and graduation rates at various levels, and within certain ages and poverty levels, and the median earnings at different levels of education.

You can assess data individually, or you can cross-filter data where you can examine by race, by population age, by degree, by income. This will help you identify opportunities and understand your target audiences.

I can also assess employment within the area. I can see what industries individuals are employed within, in sheer numbers as well as percentage distribution. I can examine the median earnings per industry and see who makes what, based on the category of employment that they're with in. A wealth of data is available.

Government generated data is also abundant. The Center for American Progress is one of many data centers in the U.S. For example, I found a report on the workplace wage gap that examined health, educational attainment, political leadership, and other factors. Based on their reporting, the population of women in the U.S. is 50.8%, approximately half. Nearly 36% of that group are women of color. They've also looked at poverty; between 10% and 26% of women are living in poverty. They've diversified it based on ethnicity as well. They've looked at education. They've looked at income. They've looked at health insurance and a variety of other factors. This provides us with insight into understanding the customer, and understanding the market, and understanding demographics within that market.

As entrepreneurs, we are not examining demographics only for general knowledge. Where are the opportunities? Is there an opportunity to do training, workforce development, education, or other activities? Where can we bring new solutions to the problems that exist?

In summary, understand that demographics provide insights into where opportunities exist now, and even more importantly, where they may exist in the future. With demographics, we're better equipped to develop appropriate business and marketing strategies to target the customers that we want to focus on.

What psychographics changes are creating new market opportunities?

While many of us are familiar with demographics, the concept of *psychographics* is new to most. We will explore psychographics as it's related to macroeconomic change, and what we can do with this knowledge to be better entrepreneurs. This is the second element that we're examining within our discussion of macroeconomic change.

Our definition of psychographics is the attitudes, values, opinions, interests, and related personal factors of markets. It's contrasted with demographics in that psychographics involve how people think, how they feel, and their interests and values. It's influenced by their social class, lifestyle, and personality.

Most of us, as individuals, are primarily concerned with basic health and wellness—the food and shelter elements. We go from there into safety, esteem, and on up through actualization and transcendence. There's a pattern that we see of human behavior and human needs and wants.

To understand psychographics, there are a variety of resources. One of the better ones is Nielsen's MyBestSegments, which provides dozens of audience profiles. You may find profile 04, which is a *Wealthy Younger Family Mix*, and Nielsen has categorized this group as tech-savvy, fashionable, urban fringe, relatively affluent, highly educated, and ethnically mixed. These are communities with trendy apartments and condos, fitness clubs, boutiques, casual restaurants and bars from juice to coffee to microbrews. This characterization tends to be centered on urban areas—New York, Philadelphia, D.C., Chicago, L.A., San Francisco, and other pockets as well. The top five densest counties include Arlington and Alexandria in Virginia, New York City, D.C., and San Francisco, and when we dive deeper to understand the statistics of this psychographic, we see U.S. households represent 1.5 million; average household income is $90,000. We can learn about where they shop, where they travel, what they read, what they watch, and what they drive.

Psychographics help us understand how and where to position our product or service. Where do we need to advertise? As we build our brand, are there other brands that are having success with our target audience? What are the characteristics and personalities of those brands? What inspiration may we draw from them?

Experiences are becoming the predominant economic offering of many innovative ventures. It's not only the item you buy. It's not only the service. It's the customization and personalization that's desirable.

In summary, understanding psychographics, in addition to demographics, provides insights into how prospective customers think and feel, and what influences their buying preferences. By examining psychographics, you can gain valuable insight into the evolving needs and wants of your target customers. It also gives you insights on how to build and market your offerings effectively and efficiently.

What technical advancements are creating new market opportunities?

Technical advancements are a great source of opportunity as well. We're exploring this at a macroeconomic level as the third element of macroeconomic change.

With technical advancements, we're addressing improvements in technical processes, methods, or knowledge. It's one of the most important triggers of change for entrepreneurship. New technology enables limitless opportunities for derivative innovations.

For example, the Apple iPhone brought great value not only as a communications device and as a revenue opportunity for Apple, but for carriers such as AT&T, Verizon, and others. It also brought tremendous opportunities to the app developers who could place their apps on the iPhone. While there are many large competitors that are in the apps space, there are also countless entrepreneurs and small companies that are bringing successful apps to market. The creation of the iPhone has driven the success of many entrepreneurs and small companies through the apps that have been built for the iPhone.

As illustrated here, technical advances are great opportunities for entrepreneurs. The magnitude of the change is important, and significant change can create entirely new markets.

We also want to think about different uses for technology. We may find technologies that can be applied in many different ways.

Technical advancements can change industry dynamics and open new markets. When you have an app platform that entrepreneurs can sell into, you can work directly with Apple. Or you can even build your own independent site; sell directly to customers.

As of this writing, when we look what's the next big thing, people believe it will be Google Glass. The basic device can be fitted to the existing glasses that you may wear, or conversely, it could have an additional add-on with a nosepiece and the elements that wrap around your brow. Perhaps it will be the smartphone replacement.

We can do a variety of tasks via voice command. Wearing your Google Glass, you can look at a product. You can speak a command to scan the bar code. Within your field of vision, Google Glass can display the product description, product reviews, and competing price points online and in local stores. You can even place your order for the product, if you wish, and pay for the product via Google Glass.

I would not suggest that most of us have the expertise or the resources to build a competitor to Google Glass. But if you're interested in how to participate in that growth, the app market could be a mode of entry in developing apps for Google Glass, and trying to ride that growth curve.

You may even be too late. We see that the fitness gadgets really hit the market and grew in a big way in recent years. And Google Glass is not necessarily news anymore. It's something that's been out since May 2014. And it's something for which more products are coming to market—complementary products and complementary apps. And the big companies like Ebay and others are developing things for it as well. We may need to even think a step ahead.

The Apple Watch is something that, again, has been talked about for a while. Announced by Tim Cook on September 9, 2014, it has fitness tracking and health-oriented capabilities, as well as integration with iOS and existing Apple products and services. The first Apple Watch was available in three models, with a wide variety of case and band options. The first Apple Watch was compatible with the iPhone 5 and later iPhone models running iOS 8.2. The device was initially released in 2015.

The Apple Watch used Apple's new S1 processor, advertised as "an entire computer architecture on a single chip." It also used a linear actuator called the Taptic Engine to provide haptic feedback when an alert or a notification is received. The watch was equipped with a built-in heart rate sensor, which used infrared and visible-light LEDs and photodiodes.

Incidentally, it's not the original smart watch. That would be the 1977 HP that came to market and was an early calculator watch. It was priced at $600. Now, it's a collector's item. On Ebay, the price is upwards of $14,000.

Figure 13. HP-01 Smartwatch Designed in 1977

There are often new products that come to market that we think are new, but they are actually evolutions of past products.

Review patent applications to gain insights, and read blogs and rumor sites to see what's next.

It's valuable to think towards the future as you're exploring entrepreneurial ideas. Seek to understand trends, and try and predict what's going to happen. Think about opportunities, and begin acting on opportunities before they're late news or common knowledge. How can you shape inventions and innovations, and be at the forefront of new products and services?

Alternatively, we may be left behind. We may be left chasing existing markets. We may be left battling against industries or markets that are being dominated by others that are incumbents or that acted with better foresight. By being more proactive and by thinking about the future, we can leverage these technical advancements and be early movers.

What societal changes are creating new market opportunities?

Societal changes are a rich source of entrepreneurial opportunities as well. This is the fourth element that we're going to examine within macroeconomic change in the Opportunity Analysis Canvas.

As we define societal changes, we're exploring the social and cultural aspects of the macro-environment that affect customer needs and market sizes. This includes issues like health consciousness, career attitudes, and an emphasis on safety.

In a study by *The Atlantic*, they looked at the increasing longevity in the U.S., and that the number of Americans over 60 will increase by 70% by 2025. They looked at technology in smart machines, and how workplace automation is killing repetitive jobs and may even replace more skilled jobs, including accounting and law. When we look at the computational world, we recognize that data gives us the ability to see things on a scale that's been impossible before. When we look at new media ecology, we want to recognize visual communication as becoming a new vernacular. We want to look at super structured organizations and social tools that allow organizations to work at extreme scales. And we want to recognize the global connectivity of the world, and that job creation and innovation and political power is going far beyond the U.S. and Europe.

What this means for work skills, and where the opportunities may be for us as entrepreneurs, involves things like sense making and social intelligence, and novel and adaptive thinking. We need to build our competencies cross-culturally in computational thinking and new media literacy. We want to leverage virtual collaboration, transdisciplinary thinking, and a design mindsight, and manage an increasingly larger and more complex cognitive load.

As we think about entrepreneurs and those that will follow us, we ask, why aren't more young Americans seeking careers in innovation? In a study by MIT and the Lemelson Foundation in 2012, they examined a variety of factors. They found that 22% of the polled 16 to 25 year-olds said they'd be motivated by jobs that would give them a chance to change the world, and that 47% believe that a lack of innovation will hurt the U.S. economy.

When you dive into what types of innovations they would want to contribute to, they show a high interest in consumer products and health sciences. In web-based innovations there's high interest. We see interest in environmental invention. There's high interest in the performing arts as well.

When they assess their preparedness for careers in innovation, 45% of the respondents believed that STEM (science, technology, engineering and math) is not given enough attention in their schooling. Nearly 34% felt unfamiliar with the career opportunities in STEM. Approximately 30% thought that STEM careers were too difficult; perhaps they're influenced by the other factors of limited awareness and limited knowledge.

What can entrepreneurs do about it? These students shared an interest in having more invention and innovation projects in their education. There was interest in a place for innovation, a place to work on projects, a laboratory-like environment for ideas and innovation. There was a call for courses that would help them develop their innovation skills and creativity. Perhaps new online courses can assist them. Perhaps hands-on training and mentoring with STEM professionals is a solution. There are a variety of new venture opportunities to serve these students.

In summary, when we think about societal changes, recognize that the customer's needs and wants evolve. With that evolution there is an opportunity for the emergence of new ventures started by entrepreneurs. We also want to anticipate societal change. We want to recognize that entrepreneurs who anticipate such changes are going to play a more successful role in entering and growing and scaling their new ventures in these spaces.

What political and regulatory forces are creating new market opportunities?

When we look at *political and regulatory forces*, we'll find that they can be a hurdle, or they may present opportunities for us as entrepreneurs. We're going to look at these two forces in the context of macroeconomic change and think about how we can use these to our advantage in the creation, launch, and growth of our new ventures. Political and regulatory forces conclude our discussion of the macroeconomic change section of the Opportunity Analysis Canvas.

We'll examine how the government, including local, state, federal, and international laws and policies, influence economies, industries, and markets. Examples of these include tax policy and fiscal policy, laws regarding business law and labor law and environmental laws, as well as trade control and tariffs, and political stability or instability.

An example of these laws is crowdfunding, which is something that's attracting a lot of attention in the U.S., Europe, and other areas as well. You may be familiar with crowdfunding as applied to Kickstarter, IndieGoGo, and other platforms that are not really investment in nature. What happens with Kickstarter, if you're not familiar, is that you may go on and pre-buy a product. Companies engage in pre-sales, meaning they're going to sell a product, but it may take six months to deliver that product. They may give you as a buyer a discount as an incentive for you to be patient with that delivery, and they may need that funding that you've contributed for them to build the product.

What we're calling crowdfunding is different. We're discussing investment, where a contribution of money results in receiving equity, stock, or ownership in the company. The element that makes that different from Kickstarter is that in most countries it's illegal to go online and raise money from individuals, unless you have the proper vetting and certification from the government.

Today, companies like CircleUp and others present opportunities for the accredited investor – a high net worth individual – to invest in entrepreneurs. As an accredited investor, I can review the companies that are soliciting investors. I can learn about the company and their technology, and what their successes and ambitions are. I can make contact and certify that I am accredited.

There are thoughts on how you evolve that and expand it, and go beyond accredited investors? In the U.S., an accredited investor is an individual who has a net worth of over one million dollars, excluding equity in their primary residence, or one who has annual income in excess of $200,000 for two consecutive years.

The 2012 Jobs Act suggests there are thoughts on changing those laws. There are laws that are already beginning to take effect, such as raising the number of individuals who can participate in funding a startup from 500 to 2,000. But the bigger piece of the Jobs Act is lifting the general solicitation ban tied to accredited investors. And what that means, if enacted, is that you and I as individuals, even if we're not high net worth, can invest in startups. We may be able to buy a small percentage of that startup, maybe it's a tenth of 1%, for a few hundred dollars.

When we research equity crowdfunding, and efforts to increase the number of individuals who can participate in funding companies, there is level of skepticism and concern about the idea. The primary concern is what's to stop entrepreneurs from fraudulently raising money. What's to stop someone from making false claims, and collecting money with no real desire or expectation to use that money as intended? There are concerns for consumer protection – the protection of the individuals who are funding these new ventures.

In Europe and other areas, there are various examinations or certifications or credentials that are investor qualifiers, and unrelated to the worth of an individual. They educate prospective investors on the risks that they are taking. For individuals who pass these certifications or have these credentials, they are able to invest in startups even if they don't meet the net worth criteria that we have here in the U.S.

In the U.S., I expect there'll be a measure of certification and examination of investors to make them fully aware that investing in a startup is a risky proposition. It's riskier than the stock market and riskier than most investments they've made.

Another view of political and regulatory factors is to see government as a customer. In the Washington, D.C. area, where I live, this is a very common activity. The government buys goods and services, and they promote the opportunity for companies, to include small companies, to sell them these goods and services. There are various federal agencies that post these opportunities online in the U.S., and I expect in other regions of the world as well, that let entrepreneurs share in being a product or service provider to the government.

For example, the U.S. Department of Education offers a variety of supplier opportunities, many of which may have set aside funding—meaning reserved funding—for small businesses, women-owned businesses, minority businesses, and other special categories.

In summary, we want to understand political and regulatory factors from a few different perspectives. We want to know how the laws impact the businesses that we're in, or that we may enter. We want to build an awareness of these political and regulatory changes and forces. We want to think about government as a customer and where opportunities may emerge. This allows us to prepare, anticipate, and position ourselves to be successful, and to think differently about what we're doing, rather than falling victim to something that we may read in the newspaper or that we may learn about after the fact.

What resources are best to research macroeconomic changes?

While the resources discussed in the industry analysis section are also valuable to research macroeconomic changes, explore this list of resources for market size estimations and competitive research:

- Eurostat European Census and Statistics:
    - Click on "Statistics" for overall country demographics.
    - Use for market size estimations.
- SBDC Small Businesses Market Information:
    - Click "Market Research" to see if your industry is listed.
    - Contains market demographic information, market size, and other useful market statistics.
- US Census - US Population Estimations and Statistics:
    - Sort by state and other parameters relevant to your industry or target market.
    - Useful for market size estimations.
- Claritas US Market Segments by Zip Code:
    - Use the "Zip Code Lookup" feature to get market demographic information by zip code for common market segments.
    - Use the "PRIZM" feature on the left hand side for common segments or explore general segments via the menu at the top of the page.

Entrepreneur Spotlight on Richard Lowenthal, Founder and Chief Technical Officer of ChargePoint

The rapid rise of electric vehicles is at the intersection of multiple macroeconomic changes. Consumer demand for fuel cost savings is augmented by early adopters' interest in environmentally friendly vehicles. Many governments are providing tax incentives for electric vehicles purchases, and cities are beginning to create traffic zones that prohibit vehicles unless they are electric.

In 2007, Richard Lowenthal recognized this emerging shift in transportation and the critical need for fast, reliable charging stations. He believed that a comprehensive network of charging stations was a vital prerequisite to consumer adoption of electric vehicle and a cornerstone of the electric vehicle ecosystem.

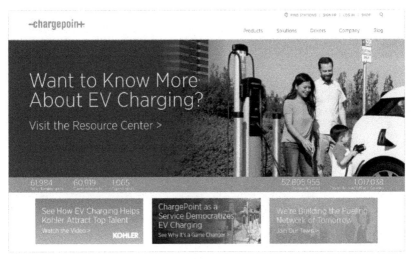

Figure 14. ChargePoint Website

After a successful career in high tech at StrataCom and Stardent Computers, Lowenthal attributes an early visit to electric vehicle pioneer Tesla Motors as the inspiration for him to launch ChargePoint. With a $15 million grant from the U.S. Department of Energy and $80 million in venture capital, ChargePoint has grown from offering single, home-based charging stations into a gas station model that serves multiple vehicles simultaneously from a single circuit.[14]

With nearly 62,000 charging spots, ChargePoint is a market leader in this growing space. By hosting over 52 million charging sessions, consumers have saved 40 million gallons of gas and driven more than 1 billion gas-free miles.[15]

[14] van Diggelen, A. (10, June 28). "Richard Lowenthal: Tesla, range anxiety & the role of charging stations." www.freshdialogues.com.
[15] ChargePoint (2018). "ChargePoint Ushers in Electric Fleet Future with Acquisition of Fleet and Energy Management Innovator." www.chargepoint.com.

Ideas in Action: Macroeconomic Change

With an understanding of how the needs and wants of your target customer influences their purchasing decisions of products and services, this activity challenges you to explore macroeconomic changes as the sixth step of the Opportunity Analysis Canvas. Your answers should be personalized based on your own interests and ambitions.

What demographic changes are creating business opportunities for new ventures?	
What psychographic changes are creating business opportunities for new ventures?	

How can you stay current on technical advancements that are emerging?	
How can you stay current on societal changes that are emerging?	
How can you stay current on political and regulatory changes that are emerging?	

Chapter 12. Competition

You have to have an international reference of competition.
You have to have the highest [standards].
Carlos Slim Helu
Mexican business magnate, investor, and philanthropist.

Assessing industry condition and industry status provides a starting point for understanding competition. To outperform the competition, the *learning curve, complementary assets,* and *reputation effects* are key factors for entrepreneurs to understand. This is the competition element of the Opportunity Analysis Canvas.

The Opportunity Analysis Canvas
Emphasis on "Competition"

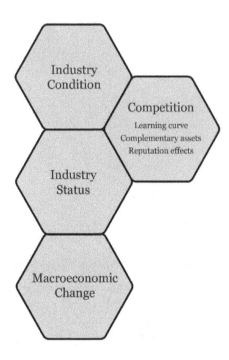

Industry Condition

Competition

Learning curve
Complementary assets
Reputation effects

Industry Status

Macroeconomic Change

How does the learning curve influence your success?

When we define a *learning curve*, we're exploring the rate of learning over time. How long does it take to get good at something?

For a simple game, such as the Angry Birds app, it's probably an hour or two. Once you understand the basic principles of the game, you can build reasonable proficiency.

There are other things that take longer. To be a world-class tennis player, it takes about 15 years. Since you reach your physical peak by your early 20s, you need to start playing by 5 years old. It takes a long time to be world class.

Learning curves are influenced by what you know today, your commitment, and your resources for learning.

When we ask who would have a learning curve advantage, it's typically the large companies. A large company that's been there and done it, and has learned from their mistakes, has grown from trial and error, and has built expertise, is certainly going to have an advantage over the new entrant and the entrepreneur who hasn't had those experiences.

There's a lot that can be learned from companies and customers. I will caution you from trying to do the same thing as a large company, because they probably have learned how to do it, and how to do it well.

How do the *Fortune 500* and IPO market improve our understanding of learning curves?

Fortune magazine publishes the *Fortune 500* list annually, which is the 500 largest revenue generating companies. If we look at those companies in 1955, we see that of the *Fortune 500* in that year, roughly half of them were still on the list 25 years later. They remained competitive, and they remained among the largest 500 companies, for 25 years.

Of the 1965 companies, approximately half were still on the list 22 years later.

In 1975, half of them were still on the list approximately 16 years later.

In 1995, when we look at a more current edition, roughly 12 years passed, with half of them still on the list.

This downward trend from 25 years to 22 to 16 to 12 evidences that maintaining your competitiveness long-term is a challenge, even for the largest companies in the world. While a few large companies have sustained – Exxon Mobil, General Electric, General Motors, etc. – the overwhelming majority of these companies have declined.

For entrepreneurs, this is an encouraging sign. Today's largest companies are susceptible to new, innovative startups. They may be replaced with new industries and new markets and new technologies.

We can also examine the initial public offering (IPO) history of companies in the U.S. How long does it take to grow to be a $100 million or $200 million revenue generating company, and IPO? In the late 1990s, during the dot-com boom, it was only four or five years. By the early 2000s, the speed of IPOs declined dramatically, and they're still relatively conservative today versus historic numbers. We see peaks of 14 and 15 years from company creation to IPO in 2007 and 2008. More recently, we see an average of 10 years for these companies. It takes time to build expertise and success, even as a fast-paced, tech company.

How is learning changing from its traditional model?

We also see evolving models for climbing the learning curve. What we call traditional learning is largely bundled in a one-size-fits-all model. There are traditional assessments and exams on a set schedule administered to all students within a class.

New stages of learning models are coming to market.

Stage one is online and blended learning (with face-to-face and online elements). A traditional financial model that is tuition-based still exists.

Stage two involves a level of unbundling, with a semi-customized curriculum. Courses may be separated into mini-courses offered at lower costs, in an online or blended format.

Stages three, four, and five continue to gravitate towards free-range learning that's transformed into unbundled that's more value focused, that's more applied, with differentiated business models.

Coursera and the MOOCs are certainly moving through this path at a fast rate by partnering with universities. We see learning based on competence building.

As you're climbing the learning curve, there are abundant resources provided by universities, companies, governments, and organizations that can give you insights into understanding markets and industries.

In summary, embrace learning to climb the learning curve. Keep in mind that the learning curve is to your advantage when you're exploring new industries, new markets, or new technologies. Focus on being different, developing innovate products and services, and incorporating customer feedback to climb the learning curve quickly.

What complementary assets influence your success?

Complementary assets, our second topic within competition, are the capabilities and/or infrastructure that support commercialization, beyond the assets associated with the product or service itself.

Complementary assets can be tangible or intangible.

It can be money. It can be equipment. It can be real estate.

The intangible assets include your knowledge and relationships, and your intellectual property – patents, trademarks, copyrights, and trade secrets. Entrepreneurs can develop an advantage if they have significant intangible assets – if they have the knowledge, the relationships, and the intellectual property. These are more difficult to replicate than the tangible assets.

How do you build your complementary assets? If you need to fulfill orders generated from your online retail site, you may buy or rent a warehouse. You may hire staff. You may manage all of your operations. Alternatively, you may partner with Amazon for inventory management and order fulfillment; without you having to build that system yourself. Or you may hire or collaborate with other partners to build your complimentary assets.

Complementary assets may increase demand, improve your commercialization, and increase the benefit or the utility of what it is you're bringing to the market.

In the consumer electronics market, there are a variety of complementary assets in place.

Sony's inclusion of Blu-ray DVD playing capabilities in their PlayStation increased the utility of their gaming console, providing significant product differentiation from the competing Microsoft Xbox.

Netflix's partnerships with Sony, Microsoft, and Nintendo enabled streaming of Netflix movies and television though these gaming consoles. While the video content itself did not change, the ease of access and improved viewing experience (versus a computer) was the result of complimentary assets in action.

Complementary assets themselves can be a source of new venture opportunities. For example, revenues for the accessories market for Apple's products exceeds $11 billion annually.

In summary, when we think about where and how we want to compete, avoid situations where the company with the most money is going to win. Instead, think about opportunities where complementary assets, and specifically, the elements of knowledge, relationships, and intellectual property, can be developed by you as a startup.

How does the reputation of competitors influence your success?

The *reputation* of competitors is important to understand. This will conclude our discussion of competition as part of the Opportunity Analysis Canvas.

Reputation is the set of generally held beliefs or opinions. This matters because customers often prefer to buy either from companies from which they've had a transaction before, or companies that they have familiarity and insight on via friends, or family, or the branding of those companies.

Today, there are an almost limitless number of online resources that shape and influence reputation. There are consumer review sites, free sites, paid sites, and professional review sites—a variety of resources that we want to be familiar with, and think about how to use, as we are doing our competitive analysis, as well as our own reputation management.

For example, we'll take a look at a company that is producing a line of educational toys called GoldieBlox. Their target customers are girls in kindergarten and elementary school. These educational toys focus on engineering, math, and science principles. They've gotten a lot of very positive press in the U.S. for encouraging STEM-based education of young women.

Figure 15. GoldieBlox Product on Amazon.com

We can look at Amazon on a product-by-product basis and understand what GoldieBlox is doing well, what they may be doing wrong, and the opinions of consumers. We can explore the product reviews and ratings to learn what people are saying about the product and about the company.

With hundreds of reviews on Amazon, we can review the highly-satisfied customers providing four-star and five-star ratings. But if we're considering entering the space, and how we can improve on it and deliver better value, it's those one-star and two-star reviews that I'd be interested in reading. We need to understand where the gaps and vulnerabilities are for GoldieBlox.

We can also study professional reviews. Sites like CNET review consumer electronics. There are many professional product review sites that provide detailed analyses that may be complemented by video, pictures, and other analytics on what professionals think about products or services.

We also want to do passive research, by which I mean automated. You can subscribe to your competitors' sites. You can subscribe and like their Facebook groups. You can set up Google Alerts. You can join your competitors via Twitter. You can use RSS feeds on certain sites, and see what's going on in the space, and set keyword alerts on your competitors or on certain products and brands that they own. For a number of these tools, you can subscribe to a daily email that provides a summary of news and information on competitors and their products.

In summary, when we think about reputation, we need to examine our competitor's vulnerabilities. Where is it that we can make an impact? Are there problems in the marketplace that we can help solve with our ventures? We also want to think about new industries and new markets that we can enter. Also think about managing your own reputation. What can we do to build and manage our reputation? We need to take an active role in setting up our own alerts to see what's being said about us, and play an active role in shaping that conversation.

Entrepreneur Spotlight on George Weinmann, Founder and CEO of Mega Maldives Airlines

With a degree in aerospace engineering and an early career with Boeing, George Weinmann's aspirations for starting a new airline were bold and challenging. With a vision to start China's first low-cost carrier, after securing millions of dollars from investors and moving to China, China curtailed foreign investment in aviation. He had to abandon the plan when it became clear that China would not approve a new airline.

Mega Maldives Airlines was soon conceived during George's honeymoon to the Maldives. He met with Maldives officials to discuss possibilities for charter operations from China. Instead, they proposed that he establish his own airline in the Maldives.

"Over the next ten years, the Maldives can become the playground in the backyard of India and China, similar to the way the Caribbean is to the U.S.A. and Canada," says George. By linking the increasingly affluent China with the Maldives, a tiny island nation, the right ingredients are in place, to include landing rights in an expanding market, an international network of contacts, and crucial government approvals.[16]

Mega Maldives flights began in 2011 with one Boeing 767 flying from Hong Kong to the Maldives. By 2016, Mega Maldives grew to 400 employees.

As is the case for a number of startup companies, the success of Mega Maldives was short-lived. Attributed to a significant decline in leisure travel by the Chinese, political unrest, and the resulting failure to secure new investment to pursue new strategies, Mega Maldives suspended all operations in May 2017.

---

[16] Gluckman, R. (2012, March 26). "A startup airline finds its place in the Maldives." New York Times Dealbook. Available at http://dealbook.nytimes.com/2012/03/26/a-startup-airline-finds-its-place-in-the-maldives/?_r=0

Ideas in Action: Competition

With an understanding of competition influences entrepreneurial opportunities, this activity challenges you to explore competition as the seventh step of the Opportunity Analysis Canvas. Your answers should be personalized based on your own interests and ambitions.

What is the learning curve in your industry and market of interest?	
What complementary assets are most critical in your industry and market of interest?	

How does the reputation of competitors influence your success?	

Chapter 13: Part III – Acting Entrepreneurially

Value Innovation
Opportunity Identification

With an understanding of *entrepreneurial mindset, entrepreneurial motivation*, and *entrepreneurial behavior*, and insights into the key industry and market forces, you are well prepared to develop your entrepreneurial ideas. Our final chapters on *value innovation* and *opportunity identification* conclude our discussion of the Opportunity Analysis Canvas.

The Opportunity Analysis Canvas
Emphasis on "Part III – Acting Entrepreneurially"

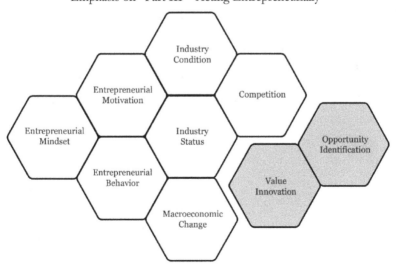

Chapter 14. Value Innovation

We didn't reinvent the circus.
We repackaged it in a much more modern way.
Guy Laliberté
Founder of Cirque du Soliel

With big ideas and scarce resources, entrepreneurs must be efficient in their decisions and discerning in their management of time and money. The concept of *value innovation* is well suited to evaluating how to compete efficiently and effectively.

The Opportunity Analysis Canvas
Emphasis on "Value Innovation"

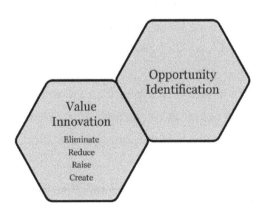

What is value innovation?

Value innovation is the parallel pursuit of product differentiation and low cost, creating a rise in value for both buyers and the company (your startup). The value to buyers is derived from the product's benefits minus its price. The value realized by the company is generated from the product's price (company revenues) minus your cost (company expenses). Value innovation is achieved when the whole system of benefits, price, and cost is aligned.

Value innovation and value curves are linked, as discussed in the article *Charting Your Company's Future.*[17] Value curves are the tool for developing and delivering value innovation. The value curve is a diagram that compares certain product or service factors on a relative scale of low to high. Factors often include features, benefits, price, brand, location, and a variety of other factors seen by customers. Diagramming each competitor's value curve alongside one another can identify value gaps, and highlight opportunities for entrepreneurs.

What value innovation opportunities are there for law firms?

For illustration, consider a traditional law firm. They are often based in opulent offices and expensive neighborhoods. They deliver a high quality of work based on their attorneys, which are very well educated, very well credentialed, and very well compensated.

Traditional law firms are expensive to hire. Legal costs are among the largest expenses of startups. Entrepreneurs may hire attorneys to assist with their corporation formation, operating

---

[17] Kim, W.C. & Mauborgne, R. (2002, June). "Charting your company's future." Harvard Business Review.

agreements, employment agreements, patents and trademarks, and sales contracts.

Due to the expense of law firms, entrepreneurs are increasingly turning to the Internet for their legal needs. Companies like LegalZoom and Nolo offer self-service, web-based tools and documents for entrepreneurs. As an online service, there are no opulent offices. Expensive attorneys are replaced with software and online tools that entrepreneurs complete based on prompts from the website. While the quality and customization of the contracts, filings, etc. from these online providers may be less than what a traditional law firm can offer, the cost savings for a suitable solution is compelling.

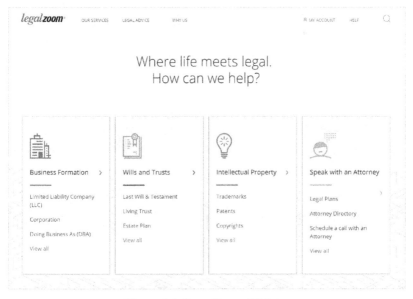

Figure 16. LegalZoom Website

These online legal services companies operate on a different value curve than traditional law firms. Experienced, talented attorneys are replaced with software. Customized services from traditional law firms are replaced with a semi-customized, template-based solution. For relatively simple, straightforward legal needs, the cost savings versus work quality equation is increasingly favoring the online providers.

As an aspiring entrepreneur that may be interested in the legal services market, starting a traditional law firm or a wholly online legal services company is ill-advised. There are significant competitors already operating on these two ends of the legal services spectrum. The alternative? Use the value curve to map where an opportunity may exist for value innovation in legal services

Perhaps I can create a new age law firm that blends an online, self-service model with limited human intervention. If customers desire a face-to-face interaction with an attorney, perhaps I can do this affordably via web conferencing in lieu of expensive office space. Or if the attorney costs are still too high, perhaps I can use legal assistants or paralegals for the interactions, and hire attorneys as supervisors.

While research and analysis is required to fully develop this idea of a new age law firm, this illustration exhibits that value curves are a valuable tool for entrepreneurs. We can consider different features, price points, and costs, and assess the positives and negatives of tradeoffs. We can create new features, and change the value proposition for customers.

What are the keys to delivering value innovation?

To deliver value innovation, focus on four questions that align with what to eliminate, reduce, raise, and create within the venture.[18] Are there select factors that we can eliminate that are

---

[18] Kim, W.C. & Mauborgne, R. (2005). Blue Ocean Strategy. Harvard Business School Press.

of limited to no real value to our target customers? A second element that we'll explore is reducing factors. Are there factors on the value curve that we can reduce without significantly reducing the value delivered to customers? Another element that we'll examine is raising certain factors. Lastly, we'll consider if there are new factors that we can create? When we look at these four questions collectively, we'll gain insights into how we can deliver value innovation to successfully compete in the marketplace.

What existing factors can you eliminate?

Your startup's elimination of factors that are delivered to customers today by competitors is certainly easier said than done. While there's the concern for eliminating factors that truly matter to customers, it is unlikely that the customer values every factor at a high level. If we can identify those factors with minimal value, we can consider eliminating them and investing our resources in those factors that add value. This give us the opportunity to deliver a faster, better, and/or cheaper solution for customers.

What is Cirque du Soleil's value innovation?

By illustration, we will explore Cirque du Soleil. Perhaps you've seen this next generation circus on their touring show. They've been very popular in Las Vegas for the last twenty years.

Cirque du Soleil made a conscious decision to eliminate factors at the conception of their company. If you are able to identify factors to eliminate, you can save the expenses of money and time. You can reinvest those resources into factors that do add true value for customers.

When we examine circuses, take a step back and think about

what the circus has been for over a hundred years. It's been reasonably affordable, and more of a family outing. It's had star performers. Animals have been a feature, as have aisle concessions. There are multiple stages, the three-ring circus if you will, where action is taking place within each ring in parallel. Clowns and fun and humor have always been a part of it, as have thrills and danger.

Cirque du Soleil eliminated most of these factors. They did away with the star performers. There are no animals. They removed aisle concessions and multiple show arenas. They still deliver fun and thrills.

Cirque du Soleil added new elements, to include a single story to present a unified them for the entire show. It is a very refined experience within each of their multiple productions. There may be a dozen Cirque du Soleil shows, each with a different theme, going on globally at any given point in time. The artistry, music, and dance of their shows deliver a very different circus experience.

They changed the value curve, and it started by eliminating what most of us perceived as the fundamental factors of the circus. They've created a whole new type of entertainment and a whole new type of experience. They've reinvented the structurally unattractive circus industry and changed those competitive dynamics. They've also challenged convention and dared to do things differently.

Cirque du Soleil changed the customer. While the traditional circus focuses on families and, specifically, children, Cirque du Soleil has changed that entirely. If you take a child, particularly a young child, to a Cirque du Soleil performance, they will likely not enjoy it. It will be awkward and weird, perhaps scary for younger children. It's clearly aimed at an adult audience.

Adults have different needs, different wants, and a different willingness to pay. Ticket prices for a Cirque du Soleil performance may be triple or quadruple your traditional circus like Barnum and Bailey. With a different market, a different feature set, a different experience, and a very different price point, Cirque du Soleil may align more with a Broadway show.

By differentiating our startup's target customer we can gain clarity on what factors to eliminate. For Cirque du Soleil's target of adults, a shifting away from the animals, the candies, the feature performers all made sense. Integrating factors from Broadway, the opera, and rock concerts aligned well with their customer.

Figure 17. Cirque du Soleil

Eliminating factors requires an understanding, and perhaps a redefinition, of the customer. Who is your target customer and what are their needs and wants? What are the competitive dynamics of your industry as related to this type of customer?

Next, we'll examine the second step of value innovation,

reducing factors.

Where can you reduce factors and not reduce value?

While select factors may be eliminated, others may be preserved, albeit reduced. These reductions present an opportunity to be more efficient and effective than competitors. Deprioritizing these less essential factors enables you to focus on the high value factors.

What is Nintendo's value innovation?

Competing directly with existing competitors is a challenge for small and large companies alike. Nintendo developed a new vision for their Wii, a new interactive game play format that abandoned the conventional keypad controller in favor of a new motion-based approach.

They envisioned an energetic experience that pulls kids off of the sofa and entices adults as well. Instead of sitting on a sofa or chair playing, as was done for decades, the Wii is an interactive environment.

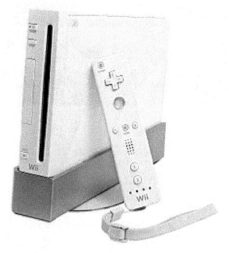

Figure 18. Nintendo Wii

They abandoned the traditional game console developer's emphasis of better graphics, faster computing power, and complex game strategies and storylines. In this way, they reduced selected factors and emphasized others to compete in a new way with Sony's PlayStation and Microsoft's X-box.

Nintendo's success with the Wii illustrates how companies can create new customer demand by engaging customers previously unserved in their product category. For Nintendo, these noncustomers were older non-gamers, parents who desired their children to be more active, and very young children. This lead to a console based on fun, simplicity, and interactivity. This reduced the need to invest in consoles that were expensive to build, expensive to sell, and expensive to develop games for.

Nintendo did not seek a better solution for an existing problem. Instead, they created new demand from new customers by focusing on new wants and needs. There are always far more noncustomers than current customers. Nintendo's ability to look across existing boundaries of competition and rethink buyer value allowed them to create a new market space where a new type of demand could be developed.

By reducing the technology, complexity, and graphics of gaming, Nintendo created a new type of customer. They attracted young children, the two, or three, or four-year-old, who did not necessarily have the dexterity, or the desire, to play the games that were being delivered by Sony and Microsoft. Nintendo also attracted older non-gamers, to include parents who desired their children to be more active.

I encourage you to think less about stealing customers from competitors, and think more about creating new customers in the market. By rethinking customer value, you have the opportunity to be different. Start with a blank page when you consider what matters to customers, instead of simply assuming that your competitors have all of the right features and benefits.

Did this reduction approach work for Nintendo? Based on sales, we see the Wii, far and away, experienced more success than the competing game consoles combined. Nintendo maintained this leadership position for a number of years. This success changed the way that Sony and Microsoft perceived their gaming consoles. While very late to the market, Sony and Microsoft did eventually bring motion-based games and accessories to the market. Nintendo had the clear advantage, focused on simplicity, and delivered an innovative, interactive experience.

With reducing factors, recognize that it gives us the opportunity to be more efficient and more effective than competitors. Consider how you can differentiate your products from competitors by reducing non-essential factors, while retaining or elevating value for customers.

Once the elimination and reduction of factors is complete, attention can turn to raising select factors.

Which factors can you raise above competitors?

Think about which factors really matter. What is really needed to exceed customer desires? How does raising new factors further differentiate us in a meaningful way versus competitors, and increase our competitive advantage? Raising these high-value factors differentiates you from competitors and improves your competitive advantage.

What is Wikipedia's value innovation?

Wikipedia's alignment of value, profit, and people propositions based on product differentiation and low cost delivered new value innovations. This online resource created new value for users and motivated the general public to embrace and assist in implementing the new strategy of collaboratively developing the written content of the Wikipedia encyclopedia.

Figure 19. Wikipedia Website

By engaging its readers and the public in developing Wikipedia's content, the company raised the timeliness and the breadth of its content. This approach presented a sustainable advantage in cost and in value versus Encyclopedia Britannica, Microsoft's Encarta offering, and existing and future competitors.

If you're under forty years old, the name Britannica probably doesn't mean anything to you. For nearly 250 years, it was the preeminent encyclopedia that was available worldwide. At its peak in 1990, they sold 120,000 volumes per year, with many more volumes being handed down through generations of families. In 2010, the last print set of Encyclopedia Britannica was sold. In that year, they sold a small fraction of what they used to sell, with only 8,000 copies at a price point of $1,395. What happened? How do you go from being a household name globally to zero?

There are a few factors that came into play. We may think it was the Internet. We may think that large companies are slow to evolve, and that Britannica was overly comfortable and ignored the digital and online revolutions. Well, that's not true in this case.

Britannica was very aware of the digital market and the transition from print to digital. In 1981, they published the world's first digital encyclopedia. In 1989, they published the world's first multimedia encyclopedia on CD ROM for use on PCs. In 1994, they launched Britannica online. 1994 pre-dates the majority of the large websites that you use. They were a very early entrant in the digital space. With a mobile app in 2000, and youth-focused mobile apps in 2010, Encyclopedia Britannica was continually at the forefront of developing premium digital content.

What did happen to them was a product called Encarta, from Microsoft. Britannica delivered a very comprehensive, very high quality product, while Encarta offered a streamlined, very inexpensive alternative. Encarta's limited multimedia element was not at all comprehensive, but it was good enough. As entrepreneurs, good enough may be exactly what we need to compete with incumbents that offer over-built and over-priced products. The typical encyclopedia consumer did not necessarily need infinite detail, and infinite accuracy, and the highest level of quality. Customers were increasingly less willing to pay for that, and that's what we found with Britannica.

Microsoft also had something else different from Britannica—other revenue streams.

Microsoft was able to almost give away Encarta, because they wanted to make money by selling the Windows platform, and Windows-compatible computers as part of that experience. Britannica's revenue streams were limited to the print copies and digital editions of their encyclopedia. Encarta was not the prize offering of Microsoft; it was an add-on, an accessory to the suite of Microsoft's software products for the home.

Encarta was not the final chapter in the story of Britannica. Wikipedia arrived a few years later.

Wikipedia changed the category. It changed the product definition of what's an encyclopedia. It brought low cost—and low in this context is zero. It created new value and covered a broader array of topics. They cover contemporary individuals, television, movies, actors, and the characters that the actors portray. The general public did not only embrace reading this new form of encyclopedia, they contributed to its creation as well, via its wiki platform. Readers are invited to be the writers. This raises the timeliness and the breadth of Wikipedia's content tremendously. As a free service without advertising, Wikipedia's sole revenue stream is donations.

The Wiki Foundation drives the delivery, monitoring, and operations of Wikipedia. Salaried staff support the infrastructure of the company and supervise the site's content. Their annual revenues are approximately $45 million. These donations are solicited from users worldwide in order to support and sustain the site. Wikipedia spends nearly $35 million of that maintaining the site, as well as other administrative and fundraising activities.

Raising select factors is a very important piece in the value innovation puzzle. Determining which factors to raise is a challenge. Britannica mistakenly believed that detail and accuracy were key desires of customers. Wikipedia realized that the timeliness of the content, as well as the breadth of topics, were more important to customers than was the infallible accuracy or the absolute comprehensiveness of content. Wikipedia's free price is obviously a key differentiator from Britannica as well.

When considering encyclopedias, we would think all four of these factors are important: accuracy, detail, timeliness, and breadth. The winning entrepreneurial companies can determine which two factors are the most important of the lot, and can focus their time and resources on significantly raising those factors to deliver the greatest value to customers.

Lastly, are there opportunities to create new factors that will satisfy customers in new ways?

What new factors can you create?

If entirely new features or benefits can be delivered by your product or service, and you are unique in this way, you are highly valuable to customers.

What is Barnes & Noble's value innovation?

When we think about the creation of new factors, book retailers are interesting to examine.

Historically, independent bookstores have been very popular. The prices were comparatively high, but they offered a very knowledgeable staff, a reasonable selection of books, a nice store ambiance, and convenient store hours.

Generations later, the mall bookstores arrived. They were more affordable and the staff may not necessarily have been as knowledgeable. The selection was small, but the popular titles were readily available. Ambience was not really there, but the stores were generally open all day and into the evening seven days per week.

Then, the big box book retailers arrived. Barnes & Noble, Borders, and their competitors brought even lower prices, staff that had reasonable knowledge, and a broad selection that was ten to twenty times larger than the mall bookstores. They brought a level of ambiance, longer store hours, and even cafes in partnerships with Starbucks and The Cheesecake Factory. Initially, these new factors brought significant competitive advantage over the mall bookstores and the independent bookstores.

But, were the big box book retailers thoughtful in the long term? Did they miss something? Were the key features that they identified the right key features? Based on Borders' later bankruptcy and financial troubles at Barnes & Noble, perhaps further factors needed to be created. Was it the online element?

While Borders and Barnes & Noble did eventually build an online presence, they were relatively late adopters compared to Amazon.com. From 2001 to 2008, Borders outsourced its online sales to Amazon, essentially handing customers over to Amazon during the emergence of online retailing.

Barnes & Noble did move quicker in the eBook reader market. They introduced the Nook in 2009, as their tablet and eBook reader competitor. This provided them with a factor that differentiated them from Borders, who had no such device until a year later. Barnes & Noble is, however, still struggling.

What do customers really want? What do they really value? Are we arbitrarily adding factors? For book retailers, what factors should they create to improve the value that they are delivering to customers and compete effectively with online retailers?

When we think about value innovation, the opportunity to

create new factors is perhaps the most feasible path to differentiating your startup from competitors. Can your new factors make the competition less relevant? What new features can you bring to the market that are unique, highly valued by customers, and sustainably competitive for you?

Think about the opportunity to create factors, raise factors, reduce factors, and eliminate factors. These are all drivers of the value curve, and critical to delivering value innovation to customers.

Entrepreneur Spotlight on Julie Uhrman, Founder and CEO of Ouya

Julie Uhrman saw opportunity in the hyper-competitive video gaming space dominated by industry titans. In July 2012, she entered her Ouya concept into the Kickstarter crowd-funding site, and in one month reached pre-sales of $8.5 million. In a field of expensive consoles and a business model unchanged for decades, she aimed to offer a very different experience.

By leveraging the Android software platform, and emphasizing low cost for the consumer instead of the high technology focus of the new Microsoft Xbox One and Sony PlayStation 4, Ouya offered a different unique selling proposition than the established competitors. With this model, new versions of Ouya will launch annually, while traditional game consoles cycle between four to six years.

Ouya's $99 price was far lower than that the $400-$500 traditional game consoles.

Figure 20. Ouya Game Console

A major differentiator from the incumbents is its open platform, enabling independent developers (and even game players) to easily make and post new games, requiring only a screwdriver to make hardware modification and add-ons. With all systems thereby being a development kit by design, any Ouya owner can be a developer without licensing fees.

Julie Uhrman's innovative product reduced or eliminated realistic graphics and superior processing power, while raising and creating new values in democratizing video gaming.

Despite the successful Kickstarter campaign and its innovations, sales of the Ouya were lackluster. The company sold its software assets to Razer, Inc., who announced the discontinuation of the Ouya console in July 2015.

Ideas in Action: Value Innovation

With an understanding of how the principles of value innovation can be applied to evaluating how to compete efficiently and effectively, this activity challenges you to consider value innovation for your target customers.

Using the principles of value innovation, what existing factors can you eliminate?	
Where can you reduce factors and not reduce value?	

Which factors can you raise to exceed customer expectations?	
What new factors can you create that will bring new values in new ways to customers?	

Chapter 15. Opportunity Identification

Older people sit down and ask, "What is it?"
but the boy asks, "What can I do with it?"
Steve Jobs
Co-founder and CEO of Apple and Pixar

Entrepreneurial opportunities become real when you have a solution that leverages your advantages to solve an important problem for customers. This chapter examines how to translate the approaches and tools of this book to act on real entrepreneurial opportunities. The key elements of opportunity identification are *defining the problem, crafting a competitive solution, building your advantage,* and *forming the right team.*

The Opportunity Analysis Canvas
Emphasis on "Opportunity Identification"

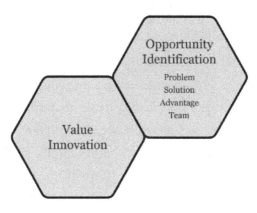

Is the problem real?

What I mean by *problem* is a problem that you seek to solve in the market. It could be an opportunity that you discovered.

What I mean by *real* is are there enough customers that really care about the problem that you aim to solve? Is it something that you can build a business on?

An early question to ask to define the problem is who is your customer? This is the first step to defining your market and understanding the problem. With this knowledge, you can focus on assessing their needs. Focus on customer value first. Why do they need your product? What benefits will they gain? Can they make money or save money with your product? These are all questions to consider in understanding the problem that you aim to solve.

Once this first round of problem-related questions are answered, the next questions are: How many people experience these problems now? In the future? How many buyers are there? Are there enough people who care about this problem for you to be financially successful by solving the problem?

With the Opportunity Analysis Canvas, your assessment of the industries, markets, competition, and value innovations are all very important to help answer this question of who is your customer and how can you best serve them.

There are typically a few customers that will buy almost anything. You need to know if there are enough customers, whether you have a real customer base, for you to be successful. Understand how many people experience that problem, now or in the future. When we forecast customer adoption of your product, note that not everyone experiencing the problem will buy your product. While a number of people may experience the problem, only a subset of them will place the economic priority on it to pay for a solution. Of those paying for a solution, a subset of those will choose your product over alternate solutions.

By illustration, we can consider two large universities in the U.S., Clemson University and Florida State University. Each has a large student base, a large alumni base, and a large fan base for their sports teams. Both do well at licensing and selling merchandise that's branded with their respective university names.

Now imagine a combination Clemson – Florida State sweater that is orange with a partial tiger logo on one side, and burgundy with a partial Seminole logo on the other side. Half of the sweater promotes one school and half promotes the other school. This is a unique and differentiated product. But is there anyone who sees value in it? Will that person be willing to pay for it?

To my knowledge, there's only one person who would wear this sweater, Ann Bowden. For a time, her husband was the head football coach of Florida State University, and her son was the head football coach of Clemson University. When the teams would play against each other once a year, she would wear a sweater that was half for one school, half for the other school. It was probably made by her, or made by a friend or family member.

Just because there is one person who is interested in that, doesn't necessarily mean that there's a market opportunity that you should pursue in mixed-school sweaters. That's what I mean by, are there enough customers?

Now the question of how many is enough feels subjective. Is it single digits? Is it thousands? Is it millions? It depends on your product and the product category. If you're developing a product at a low price point with low profit margins, you likely need to sell tens of thousands or millions of these a year to build a compelling business. Alternatively, if you're Rolls Royce or Ferrari, you may need only 2,000 customers globally in a year to develop a profitable product. Your necessary volume of customers is influenced by your financials and your cost structures.

In the pursuit of identifying real problems, I encourage you to validate the ideas that you have through customer discovery. The best way to do that is to talk with prospective customers at the start of the product development process. Engage with customers before you build a prototype, and secure their insights early on. Understand how they solve the problem that you're addressing now. Ask, what features matter? What would they pay for your solution? Use these insights to understand if there is a real problem that's worth your time to solve.

Does your solution create value for your stakeholders?

Stakeholders are individuals and organizations impacted by the product that you bring to market. Your customers are stakeholders because they buy and use your product. Your employees and advisors are stakeholders. Suppliers are stakeholders. Investors are also stakeholders.

External stakeholders also influence the success or failure of your startup. Communities, organizations, and the government may be stakeholders as well. Be aware of your stakeholders before bringing your product to market. Anticipate sources of support or resistance to your startup, and plan for how to navigate this path successfully.

By illustration, what stakeholders influence the success of a physician? Consider a small private medical practice where the physician is the owner and operator, and an entrepreneur. Their patients are the primary customers. Without customers, in this context the patients, this physician would be out of business.

Beyond patients, there are a variety of stakeholders that vary in their level of influence and relationship with the physician. For example, there are often prescriptions for medicine that physicians write. There are instruments that they use for measuring your weight and temperature, as well as surgical instruments. There are implantable devices, to include stints and pacemakers. The pharmaceutical companies, the medical supply and device manufacturers, and the distributors all play a role in healthcare.

The employers of the patients are stakeholders for the physician. In the U.S., healthcare costs are often subsidized by employers, provided that the physician completes the appropriate certifications and paperwork. This relationship is managed by healthcare benefits and insurance companies that have negotiated with employers and physicians on the prices and protocols. Employers play a role in the physician's success as a source of funding for the patients' treatments.

There are regulatory agencies, typically at the federal level, that establish the norms of medical practice. What should the physician do in terms of treatment? What can't they do? When? At what price? Regulatory agencies, normally in the form of government, play a large role in the success of physicians as well.

The networks in the hospitals that physicians either work within, or are affiliated with, are stakeholders as well. There are various facilities, outpatient centers, urgent care clinics, and public clinics that physicians are affiliated with as well.

In this context, we recognize that the most basic relationship is between the physician and the patient. There is a broader set of stakeholders that play a role in the success of physician. Particularly for physicians that own and operate private practices as entrepreneurs, they need to be smart on the issues, the concerns, and the values that are being provided to these diverse, influential stakeholders.

Entrepreneurs need to understand the role of stakeholders, and that the right partnerships and collaborations can be tremendously helpful for startups. By considering the impacts that your startup will have on stakeholders, you can develop a solution that maximizes the positive factors for all. Conversely, anticipating resistance by stakeholders to your company or your solution is valuable to understand early in the process.

Is your advantage superior and sustainable?

Building *competitive advantage* begins with developing a customer-validated perspective on the problem and your planned solution. This provides insights on where to invest your time and resources with your product. It helps you to understand how to be competitive, which requires consideration of two elements: the *degree* of your advantage and the *sustainability* of your advantage.

What is the degree of your advantage?

Are there better features that you can bring to the market? If a competing product has five features, it doesn't necessarily mean that you need those five features plus several more. Instead, focus on delivering the right set of features. From our discussion on value innovation, maybe there are one or two features that customers don't really value. You can remove those and reinvest your resources into the features most desirable by customers.

By illustration, when Ray Kroc bought a small, family-owned restaurant chain in 1961, he reduced the number of menu items, retaining only the top sellers: burgers, fries, and shakes. The limited menu was standardized with the singular goal of serving food fast. McDonald's as we know it was born on the premise of fast food, not low price food. Low prices are difficult for startups to achieve due to the economies of scale enjoyed by the large incumbents.

If your competitive advantage is based on low prices, be sure that you can accomplish this in a sustainable way, perhaps based on your operations. Where there is opportunity for a startup to offer lower prices, and if it's accompanied by cost advantages in the startup's operations, supply chain, manufacturing, etc., you can add real value for customers.

For example, consider your experience of watching movies at home. Several years ago, many of us went to Blockbuster or our local video rental place, chose our movie, paid for our movie, went home and watched the movie, and then came back a day or two later and returned that movie. Netflix brought an alternative movie rental model to the U.S. in 1997. In its beginning, Netflix was a mail order business. Customers visited Netflix.com, chose the movies that they would have selected at Blockbuster, and waited several days for the DVDs to arrive from Netflix via the U.S. Postal Service. To compensate for the wait, the movie rental rates of Netflix were cheaper than Blockbuster, and the titles were nearly always in stock. Many of us were willing to wait a few days on the mail to avoid going to Blockbuster, hoping that the movie title that we desired was available on the shelf, watch it, and then travel back to Blockbuster and return it before late fees accumulated.

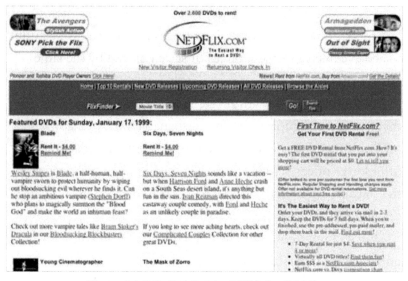

Figure 21. Netflix Original Website (1999)

While McDonald's sold speed, Netflix sold convenience and low cost by bypassing the cost of operating retail stores. Netflix did not compete on the basis of speed—at least not at first.

Blockbuster eventually launched a mail order feature and later offered online streaming of movies. They lagged competitors in both of these formats, and they still carried the expense of their bricks-and-mortar stores. Sure, they could try and copy Netflix, or copy Redbox's vending machine model. This would not help Blockbuster avoid all of the expenses that they were incurring on multi-year lease agreements on 9,000 stores nationwide with 60,000 employees. By comparison, Netflix employees nearly 7,000 today and generates over $16 billion annually. Blockbuster is bankrupt and has closed its operations.

Is your advantage sustainable?

We also want to consider the *sustainability* of your advantage. By sustainability, I'm addressing the relative difficulty for others to copy your advantage. How easily can an existing or new competitor observe what you're doing, learn from you, and apply their resources, know-how, and relationships to replicate your success?

What can you do to make your product difficult to copy? Maybe it's intellectual property in the form of patents, trademarks, or copyrights. Perhaps you can build a strong brand that resonates, that really takes hold in the marketplace. It may be relationships that you develop. It may be exclusivity agreements that you can sign with people to whom you are selling your product, or who are supplying you with parts for that product. There are a variety of ways that you can work to build entry barriers that make it difficult for those to come later and compete against you.

Consider the sources of your competitive advantage. How are you going to derive your advantage in the first place?

One way is specialization.

How can specialization create a sustainable advantage?

What I mean by specialization is the opportunity to be different than competitors.

Today, a number of my students have business ideas built on mail-order subscription boxes. Industry leaders in this area include NatureBox and Dollar Shave Club. These are models by which you as an individual will go online, pay a fixed fee per month, typically $20 to $30. You agree to an automatic mailing, typically monthly, of a box of products of a specific type or category. The mailing occurs monthly until you cancel the subscription.

For the businesses who are providing that product, it's a great revenue model. If they can convince a customer to check a box once and enter their credit card number, they know that every month until that customer cancels that they have a sale. For every customer that subscribes, they're going to have steady revenues each and every month. They can make agreements with their suppliers based on this predictable demand. They can develop a number of distribution agreements to bring in new products within their category. We see this model not only in food and shaving, but in cosmetics, apparel, wine, and educational products and craft products for kids.

As my students approach me with a new subscription box idea, a quick online search typically evidences that their idea is not new at all. As of December 2014, there were over 600 mail-order subscription box companies in the U.S. These companies often offer multiple types of boxes, resulting in thousands of options available for customers. The subscription box model has become oversaturated very quickly.

What does excite me is a company called Cratejoy based in Austin, Texas. Cratejoy does not compete to be the latest in the subscription box market. Cratejoy is one of the few companies that has made the choice to build the tool, to build the platform, to be inspired by the picks and the shovels that the gold miners needed in generations past.

Cratejoy started a software company in the summer of 2013 to support creators their own subscription box company. Those who want to be the provider of that subscription service can use Cratejoy's software platform to build a site, manage inventory, and manage payments. For a monthly fee, Cratejoy provides a fully integrated service for the hundreds of companies that are chasing the mail-order subscription market.

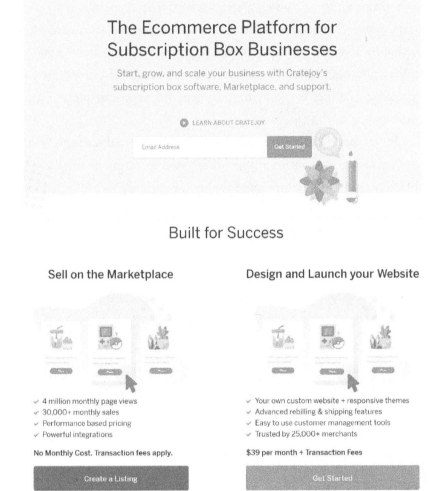

Figure 22. Cratejoy Website

Cratejoy started with two individuals with technology expertise. They applied and were accepted in Y Combinator's summer program, a leading startup accelerator. Approximately a year later, in September of 2014, they raised $4 million in venture capital to continue to build, scale, and market the business. Again, not trying to be the latest subscription box service, but trying to specialize as a tool for the emerging box service companies.

How can localization create a sustainable advantage?

Localization is another opportunity to be competitively different and build competitive advantage. We see this in international markets where there's a domestic product that's doing well. The example here would be Spotify in the U.S., which offers music in an all-you-can-listen model for a low monthly fee. There is a new competitor in Taiwan, KKBOX. While they offer the same popular music that Spotify has, KKBOX further differentiated by signing local music labels and entering into agreements that provide this company with unique access, a unique catalog of music for their local market. They're able to anticipate desires and serve individuals in their home country in a better way than a Spotify could as a non-Taiwanese company. In this context, it's specialization to an extent, but even more so, it's a localization strategy.

How does the team create a sustainable advantage?

A third source of competitive advantage is the team. If you're already successful, if you're Google or Microsoft, you can recruit great talent and great executives. Recruiting is tremendously difficult for startups, but incredibly important. As you're searching for co-founders, as you're looking for your first or second employee, you should be seeking great people. Search for people who are excellent at what they do. What you can expect is a greater likelihood of having excellent products and an excellent company if you start with an excellent team.

If I were to start an electric vehicle company, I'd like to hire a CTO, a chief technology officer, who had done great things in this space before. One who had built and scaled electric vehicle companies before, who understands complex electrical systems, who understands aerodynamics, and who understands how to build a competent technology team.

I need a chief financial officer who knows numbers, who understands money, who understands the automotive industry. The former CFO of Ford of Southern Africa, which is a $3 billion operation in and of itself, would be a good fit.

A chief designer who knows design is critical. One who has won countless awards, who has demonstrated that they can design great cars that people will buy and love. Perhaps the past director of design from Mazda's North American Design Center, one of the global centers of excellence for automotive design, who also has design experience with General Motors and Volkswagen.

I need a person that can build cars well, and build a lot of cars really well. The past production lead with Lexus, Toyota, Volvo, and Renault fits, as they've been responsible for building over 350,000 cars per year.

I need a procurement expert that understands global supply chains for manufacturing companies. The former chief purchasing officer for Sony Ericsson fits.

I want my company to be fun. I want my company to be a place where my colleagues can come and enjoy what they do, and enjoy their work, and enjoy the company culture that we can build. What better person to have than the director of staffing operations for Google, who was responsible for growing Google from their early days up until 2009, and designed the company's legendary recruitment organization and talent acquisition strategy.

Tesla Motors doesn't only build great cars. They build great teams. They built this great team in the beginning to enable their building of great cars and a great company.

In summary, think about the degree of your competitive advantage and its sustainability. Can you do something that is better, cheaper, and/or rarer than competitors? Can you build something that's sustainable and difficult to copy? And can you find sources of advantage either independently or in combination, such as specialization, localization, and teaming?

Can you build the right team at the right time?

We're going to further explore *teaming* as we conclude our discussion on opportunity identification. Entrepreneurship is a team sport. The belief that it's the solo individual out on their own all the time is a myth. Entrepreneurs spend the majority of their time as part of a group. They're meeting with management teams, board members, and project teams. And as the venture grows, they're spending more and more time with suppliers, partners, and customers.

How do startups build teams? How do you pick your co-founders? How do you pick your earliest employees?

Thoughtfully consider who has complimentary interests. Who likes what I like and who has the passion for what I want to do?

Who has contrasting skill sets? Who are people that know things different than me? Who can complement my weaknesses with their strengths?

Are there differentiated relationships among my team? Will my team members know more people, and different people?

Think about your reasons for teaming. You may want to expand or enhance your industry knowledge or domain knowledge. You may want to bring someone to the team that understands the customer and the market, and who understands the competitors and trends. You may want someone who has the relationships and the social capital. The person who's in the know, and knows who to know.

You may want someone who can make a financial contribution. Now, maybe they are an investor, and only an investor. Maybe they are an investor and they're going to be working with the team in a more day-to-day fashion as well.

Should you team with a close friend to start your business? Or bring them on early in the venture? I would caution you that many times, teaming with friends usually ends the friendship and kills the business.

There are two questions that I would ask. One, does your friend truly complement your strengths and weaknesses? Two, if you had the money to hire someone into that role, would you hire that friend? If the answer to either of these questions is no, then that's not a friend that I would bring on to the team.

What is the best approach to team building?

An ideal approach is to start with people you know. Only hire people you know. Particularly as a small team, having a bad hire may be the end of your company. It's time and money spent that may be irrecoverable.

Find partners with resources who can commit long-term. Find individuals who are willing not to take a salary for a period of months or even years: who have the savings that they can support themselves through the initial growth and scaling of the venture.

Find people who have experience.

Integrate people with sales and marketing very early in the process.

Staff your group with people who believe in your mission that aren't only exploring for salary.

While all of the above may be ideal, it's not the reality of most startups.

The majority of the entrepreneurs with whom I advise are first time entrepreneurs. Typically, they do not know the right people. They have not worked in the companies, or joined programs, that connected them with the right people. They are not wealthy, and neither are their friends. And they are unable to afford experienced hires for their startup.

Be sure to identify the skills that your new venture needs. This takes an honest self-assessment of what you know, what you don't know, and what's critical to your venture.

If you're starting a technology-based venture, I suggest bringing on technology talent in a co-founder or full time management position. Beware outsourcing your core capabilities.

Recruit through a variety of means. You may have friends who have the right skill set. If they are committed, and have the right skills, complementary interests, and differentiated relationships, they may be a compelling team member.

Past or present co-workers can be great team members as well. You know their expertise. You know their work ethic. You know their personalities, and if you enjoy working with them.

Family members with the right skills, motivations, and relationships can be valuable team members. However, if you have family who may not be the most reliable, and have problems in their day-to-day life, I would be hesitant to bring them on to the team. Be highly selective.

LinkedIn, Facebook and other social networks can be very helpful for finding individuals. LinkedIn, by being able to index people on expertise, education, and experience, is a great tool to find people. There may be people who were in your circle years ago who have gone on to do pretty impressive things that you may not be aware of. If you connected on LinkedIn, you may find that they're the perfect co-founder, or that they're the perfect individual to join your team later.

You may recruit at face-to-face events. There are a variety of meet-ups, workshops, speakers, and socials in many different areas. They happen in many large and small cities globally, as people are more informed about entrepreneurship.

Understand the roles of cash and equity in your venture. You may be cash poor, but equity rich. What I mean by that is you may not have the cash to bring on individuals. You may not be able to pay a salary. But, every company starts with 100% equity. In that context, you have 100% ownership of your company to perhaps share with people who will join your team. Consider what it takes to bring people on and effective ways to bring them on with equity. Consider a vesting schedule to engage and retain them with your venture.

We also want to create a strong culture by hiring people whom you like to work with, and who share your values. Those who you think can be long term advocates and champions of your venture, of your cause, and of the solutions that you want to bring to market.

There's also an extended team. The extended team may be your board. It may be investors, attorneys, accountants, partners, and suppliers.

The extended team is something to be cautious about as well. Hopefully, if you were to choose a physician, you're not just going to flip through the yellow pages or search "physician" on the Internet and pick the first person who comes up and trust them with your healthcare. However, many entrepreneurs do that when they're searching for attorneys or accountants. That's not the thing to do. Do the same thing you would do if you were trying to find a physician. Look for people who are respected, who have references, who may have worked with other individuals whom you know. I would be as selective with my extended team members as I would be for my own personal physician.

Why is a board of advisors critical for your success?

A key piece of the extended team is the board of advisors. It gives you a mechanism to have regular feedback from people who have expertise and insights, and who can provide an objective and informed level of feedback.

A board of advisors doesn't have a formal role or a formal influence over you. It's very different from a board of directors, who may have the legal ability to hire or fire the executive team, who may have the ability to choose to spend or not to spend on large scale projects, who may have the ability to approve or not approve acquisitions or mergers. Boards of directors often have considerable obligations and authority. Boards of advisors simply advise. And for the early stage entrepreneurs, that's what I would suggest starting with. It gives you a rich source of advice that long-term should help you make money, and should also save you a lot of money and save you from mistakes and pitfalls along the way.

A board of advisors is also different from a service provider. If you go to a marketing firm and you want them to market your product, they will create a campaign. They will suggest what may work. They will attach a price point to it. And they're happy for you to pay them $1,000 or $10,000 or $50,000 for them to execute that marketing plan. A board of advisor member is able to work with you on that plan, and will ask if it's going to work or not? What should you do? What shouldn't you do? What are other non-marketing things that you can do with that $10,000 that may add more value to your firm?

If you go to a software development company and ask them to build your dream website, they will do it. They may be able to do that for $50,000. And they're happy to build it. They'll provide no guarantees that it's going to be profitable. They'll provide no guarantees that you're going to be able to have traffic on that site and convert customers on that site, but they'll take your money to build it. A board of advisors will look at that plan, look at that wireframe, think about that user interface, think about the customer experience that that website is going to deliver, and give you advice on what to do, when to do, how to do, if to do, etc. before you hire a software development company.

Boards of advisors may be compensated. It may be equity based. It may be 0.25% to 1%. It may be cash-based. They are potentially willing to serve as a volunteer for a short amount of time, if they already have a relationship with you. I would argue that to really get value out of them, and to really have their attention, and link their interest and their motivation to you in a measurable and significant way, there's a level of equity or cash that most startups are going to need to bring on quality boards of advisors and to be a priority for them.

In summary, when we think about the team, we want to be very selective. We want to be very selective with our co-founders as well as the early hires that we make, particularly those who we are going to give equity to. We also want to be very selective with our extended team.

We want to beware the pitfalls of friends and family. Yes, there are successful companies formed by friends. There are successful companies that are run by families. But it's not the norm. And it certainly brings a level of complication that you want to be aware of.

Leverage your relationships to establish your team. Think about whom you know and if they may be a prospective teammate.

I also want to remind you of this concept of building a board of advisors. It's a great way to have expert advice, and advice is something that you can take or leave.

Ideas in Action: Opportunity Identification

To translate the approaches and tools of this book to act on real entrepreneurial opportunities, the questions challenge you to explore the ninth and final step of the Opportunity Analysis Canvas.

What evidence can you provide that your proposed problem is significant?	
What key customer values does your solution offer?	

How will you make your advantages superior and sustainable?	
What steps will you take to build the right team at the right time?	

Chapter 16. Insights on Corporate Venturing

Startups are not the only creators of innovation. In the 1970s, 3M scientists Spencer Silver and Arthur Fry were exploring uses for an adhesive that Silver had discovered. This eventually resulted in the groundbreaking product that 3M launched in 1980 and which has since become an office and household staple, the Post-It Note. In the 1990s, the Sony PlayStation started as an afterhours project for Sony Sound Engineer Ken Kutaragi. The gaming system soon became the best-selling game console of its era.

What these and other ideas had in common was that their creators benefited from a corporate setting that fostered creativity. By pursuing their own projects, these innovators were "intrapreneurs," a term coined in 1985 by Gifford and Elizabeth Pinchot to refer to "free market entrepreneurship within the corporate organization." Also called "corporate entrepreneurship," intrapreneurship involves individuals or groups of individuals exploring high-risk, high-reward ideas within a larger, established company structure.

There are two enablers of intrapreneurship:

1. Encouragement and support from the senior leadership of the company; and
2. Reassurance that even if the ideas fail, the intrapreneur will not be unduly penalized or stigmatized.

The second enabler is particularly important in today's competitive and judgmental business environment. In a recent Ernst & Young survey of 263 of the world's leading entrepreneurs (all winners of Ernst & Young's Entrepreneur of the Year awards), 82% of the respondents strongly agreed that the ability to innovate was critical to the growth of their organizations.

Innovation benefits from experimental and agile organizational structures that fuel creativity and accommodate failure. In contrast, most large established companies are comprised of rigid, hierarchical institutional structures that can stifle the entrepreneurial spirit and innovative decisions. Generating innovative ideas typically becomes more difficult as organizations grow in size and complexity.

Enterprising corporations that consider intrapreneurship as essential seek the best of both worlds. They possess the necessary financial and marketing resources to act on innovative ideas. In parallel, they often employ a vast internal talent pool available to supply and act on entrepreneurial ideas. By marrying these two aspects, companies can benefit from innovations in products, processes, services, and other avenues to grow their businesses. An entrepreneurial environment that recognizes and rewards employees' creativity also boosts employees' engagement with and loyalty to the company.

This chapter provides an overview of successful intrapreneurship practices. How do companies ignite innovation by tapping into the creativity of their existing employees? What are practical strategies to foster a culture of innovation from within the company? To explore these questions, Ernst & Young conducted a series of global surveys of senior business leaders as well as interviews with leading academics, industry authorities and winners and finalists of their Entrepreneur of the Year award. Ernst & Young identified six corporate strategies that underlie the most successful intrapreneurship efforts:

1. Set up a formal structure for intrapreneurship. Give people enough time away from their "day jobs" to work on creative ideas, but set up formal processes to make sure those ideas go somewhere.

2. Ask for ideas from employees. They have their fingers on the pulse of the marketplace. Encourage everyone from all ranks and functions to contribute to the innovation dialogue.

3. Assemble and unleash a diverse workforce. Statistical research has established that diverse viewpoints result in better ideas and better products

4. Design a career path for intrapreneurs. They tend to be nonconformists who dislike conventional administrative jobs, so look for nontraditional ways to advance their careers.

5. Explore government incentives for innovation. Ask how these can support your intrapreneurial ventures. Governments all over the world are offering new tax breaks and other incentives for research and development (R&D) — and corporations in turn are urging governments to support innovation.

6. Prepare for the pitfalls of intrapreneurship. Backing bold ideas can backfire. Be prepared to deal with failed ventures, internal conflicts, financial risks and intellectual property battles.

These guidelines provide a roadmap for establishing a supportive environment for the innovative process. This provides the foundation for institutionalizing intrapreneurship so that it becomes an inseparable part of a company's operations. This allows continuous innovation to take place and positions the company to become and stay a market leader.

1. Set up a formal structure for intrapreneurship

Formal processes typically work better in established companies than ad-hoc efforts. Many large companies generate good ideas, but fail to effectively translate these to the commercialization stage. Research shows that structured and formal processes for innovation are more likely to result in viable new ideas. In a McKinsey Global Survey of more than 2,000 executives, respondents from companies that set formal priorities for innovation were more likely to say that their firms were better at innovation than their peers. Inversely, the absence of a formal process correlated with poor performance in bringing new products and services to market.

One of the most effective ways to encourage internal innovation is to give employees sufficient time away from their day jobs to work on new projects. At 3M — ranked as one of the most innovative companies in the world — employees are encouraged to spend up to 15% of their time working on new ideas to benefit the company. If an idea is viable, the company funds it. One funding program is called the Genesis Grant, which offers employees up to $85,000 to advance their ideas. A formal panel of technical experts and scientists initially review the ideas submitted. The most promising ideas proceed to a committee of senior technical experts and company management. This group evaluates the ideas for potential competitive advantage, projects where preliminary experimental work has already been completed, and projects for which resources required from both within and outside 3M have been identified. Approximately 15 Genesis Grants are awarded each year. Products that have resulted from this program include Scotch Pop-Up Tape and 3M's multilayer optical film technology, Vikuiti, for laptop and cellular phone displays.

Google's concept of Innovation Time Off is another example of reallocating employee time towards new ideas. The goal is to encourage creativity among Google's employees and support continuous innovation. Approximately 20% of an employee's time is to be spent on company-related work that was of personal interest. Nearly 50% of Google's new-product launches — including Gmail, Google News, and AdSense — originated from the Innovation Time Off program.

Global glass and ceramics manufacturer Corning Incorporated maintains its entrepreneurial spirit by allowing scientists and engineers 10% to 15% of their time to work outside their current projects. "From the outside, we might look like a really large, process-oriented company," says Waguih Ishak, Division Vice President of Corning Incorporated and Science and Technology Director of the Corning West Technology Center in Silicon Valley. "But when you go inside, you'll see that our process rigor is grounded in an innovative and risk-taking spirit. Let's say I'm an engineer working on a new display, for example. While I'm waiting for my new prototype to be built, I can use

10% to 15% of my free time to pursue a biotech idea that uses some of the knowledge generated by the display project. I'm free to contact another business unit and find out what they need. In that way, I may produce another invention in a totally different area from the one I'm formally working in."

2. Ask for ideas from employees

Tapping the wisdom of employees is becoming an indispensable source of ideas for companies, according to Christopher Tucci, Professor of Technology Management at the Ecole Polytechnique Fédérale de Lausanne (EPFL) in Switzerland. "A digitally networked world offers the unique ability to broadcast a problem to a large group of people or community (called the 'crowd') and call for solutions," he says.

Tucci notes that "crowdsourcing" — a term coined by Wired magazine writer Jeff Howe in 2006 — can exist within companies via "internal crowdsourcing". Companies can use the knowledge base of their own employees via traditional techniques, such as ratings and feedback on R&D projects or a virtual suggestion box. Creating an "idea exchange" or "market for innovation" are newer approaches. The latter is a technique for evaluating the quality of ideas and worthiness of corporate funding.

Recent research published in MIT Sloan Management Review shows that engaging employees across all functions and ranks in "innovation communities" can lead to highly creative ideas, as well as practical suggestions for their implementation.

The research describes the case of food retailer SUPERVALU Inc., where each year approximately 40 managers separate into four teams to discuss strategic issues proposed by executives. These managers examine issues that are outside of their own areas of expertise. During a six month period they hold weekly online meetings and meet in person monthly to discuss the issues, all while continuing to perform their regular duties. At the conclusion of the six month session, they send their recommendations to company leaders, who determine which ideas to implement. Over the past 10 years recommendations have been implemented from 22 out of 29 projects completed.

At Honda Motor Company, innovation communities are comprised of employees from sales, engineering and development, and from different business units across the globe.

General Electric Company involves consumers and business clients in new product discussions as well.

Since 2001, IBM has used "Jams" — massive online brainstorming conferences — to generate innovative ideas and solve problems. The 2006 InnovationJam involved 150,000 IBM employees, business partners, clients from 67 companies, and university researchers. Participants posted ideas from 104 countries, and conversations spanned 24 hours a day. This InnovationJam resulted in $100 million being allocated to start 10 new businesses for IBM, including a 3D internet systems unit and a unit to develop and apply environmental technologies. In addition to generating new businesses for IBM, the ideas resulting from the InnovationJams sparked the company's transition from computer hardware and software company to a provider of business and technology services.

3. Assemble and unleash a diverse workforce

Academic research by Scott Page, a professor of complex systems at the University of Michigan, and others has established that diverse groups typically outperform homogeneous groups, even if the members of the latter group are more capable.

Diversity can improve an organization's performance by enhancing creativity or team problem-solving.

Researchers at Stanford University and Cornell University have shown that diversity encourages the intellectual debate and conflict that lead to innovation.

Other research supports these findings:

- In a study of 28 teams, heterogeneous teams solved complex tasks better than homogeneous teams. The diverse teams exhibited a higher level of creativity and a broader thought process.

- In a study conducted in Germany, higher levels of innovation and R&D correlated with higher levels of cultural diversity.

- In a study of 45 teams from five high-tech firms in the US, teams composed of people with different functional specialties worked more effectively with other internal teams and showed a higher product innovation rate.

- Where innovation is critical, companies should construct teams with equal proportions of men and women so that they can benefit from the most diverse talent pool.

It's no coincidence that effective leaders look to diverse perspectives to produce exceptionally creative thinking that may not occur otherwise.

Most large companies today have a diverse workforce that is globally distributed. This enormous diversity of culture and viewpoints can be fertile ground for innovation, if cultivated correctly.

Leading companies have shown that innovative products, services and business models can result directly from leveraging a diverse and global workforce. For example:

- The 1,100 employees at Google's facilities in India come from a spectrum of religious backgrounds and speak several Indian languages in addition to English. This diversity has resulted in Google Finance, Google's first innovation born in a foreign R&D center.
- PepsiCo has 50% hiring requirements for women and minorities; has an India-born woman, Indra Nooyi, as its CEO; and attributes one percentage point of PepsiCo's 7.4% revenue growth, or about $250 million, to new products inspired by diversity efforts.
- HP developed its new Latex Printing Technology through teams consisting of 120 engineers working together in four countries; the company believes that diversity of teams was critical to the project's success.
- As of 2008, Procter & Gamble had delivered, on average, 6% organic sales growth since the beginning of the decade, virtually all of it driven by innovation from diverse teams.

4. Design a career path for intrapreneurs

Intrapreneurs tend to be mavericks whose philosophies and ideas are at odds with those of the organization. Many may quit to form their own businesses, and take their ideas and innovative spirit with them.

A classic case of an intrapreneurship effort that didn't work is that of the founders of Adobe Systems, John Warnock and Charles Geschke. They believed that their new product ideas were not encouraged by their former employer. They left in the 1980s to form their own business. Today, Adobe has annual revenues of more than $3 billion.

For the intrapreneurs that remain with their employer, there are tremendous benefits from the technical, marketing, financial, and related infrastructure of a large company. For longtime Microsoft developers Robbie Bach and J. Allard, creating the Xbox game console may not have been possible without Microsoft's vast resources, infrastructure, and talent.

Large companies benefit from supporting intrapreneurs and providing incentives for them to stay. This includes a well-defined career path.

New research into intrapreneurship suggests that "companies fundamentally mismanage their innovation talent," in the view of scholars Gina Colarelli O'Connor, Andrew Corbett and Ron Pierantozzi. "Although there are plenty of great jobs in innovation, there are no careers," they write in a Harvard Business Review article. "One member of an innovation hub in a large consumer products company explains, 'I could help launch $4, $5, $6 billion businesses over the next five years, and I won't get promoted into leadership for this company.'"

According to Pierantozzi, the whole notion of a career path is inherently problematic for innovative people. "Let's say you're really good at exploring the frontiers of business, technology, whatever — you're looking for the next big thing," he says. "You nurture it until it's spun off. The only reward you get is to run the company, to become a general manager. But the people who excel at discovering and incubating new opportunity don't want to be general managers. What's more, they often lack the skills to do it well".

In the same manner that many researchers and scientists want to be technical experts and inventors, but not managers, many intrapreneurs may not aspire to senior management positions with administrative tasks. Instead, these intrapreneurs want to create and innovate.

In years past, companies that employed scientists created what they called "technical ladders," career paths that allowed technical people to do what they did best, while enabling scientists with managerial ambitions to take on administrative roles. Pierantozzi believes companies should do something similar for innovators.

Rewards are also key to recognizing and retaining intrapreneurs. 3M offers intrapreneurs awards for marketing excellence for reaching $2 million in new product sales in the U.S. or 4 million worldwide, and another award for technical innovation. Recipients are regarded as "corporate scientists". Intrapreneurs may also join technological or R&D forums where membership is a source of pride because it is by invitation only.

5. Explore government incentives for innovation

As the economic downturn deepened through late 2008 and into 2009, one of the most pressing concerns for many nations was that businesses would significantly reduce their R&D expenditures to improve their bottom line. Governments turned to spending "stimulus" money to support industries and fund infrastructure and jobs to stabilize their economies. To provide added incentive for companies to maintain their investment in innovation, and to attract new R&D activity, many governments have enhanced their R&D tax credit provisions.

The support from government in areas such as R&D and patent regulation varies significantly across the Americas, Europe, Asia, the Middle East, India and Africa. Julie Teigland, an Ernst & Young Strategic Growth Markets Leader, says that "for many companies in this region who operate cross-border, navigating

patent applications and grants or incentives for R&D can be a
challenge. It is not surprising, then, that respondents (from the
Middle East, India and Africa) chose simplifying the patent
process as one of their top three ways for governments to
encourage innovation. Attitudes toward intellectual property in
developing markets are also changing: for example, our survey
indicated that nearly two-thirds of respondents from South Africa
strongly agreed that the ability to protect intellectual property was
increasingly important, compared to just 28% of overall
responses."

While the increasing role of government in the private sector
continues to generate debate, companies shouldn't ignore the
many government-funded options for R&D and innovation,
especially those that support intrapreneurial ventures. In a recent
Ernst & Young survey of global R&D tax and incentive
practitioners, the types of incentives in use differ greatly around
the world. As the size of the economy increases, incentives for
R&D generally move from grants to a blend of policy tools that
involve grants and super deductions and, eventually, tax credits
that become part of the permanent tax policy of the country.

One of the more innovative set of policies that has emerged
in many countries in recent times is the concept of patent boxes.
Patent boxes are characterized as a tax measure where income
derived from qualifying intellectual property is typically taxed at a
lower rate than it would have been otherwise. Examples include
the Netherlands innovation box, with an effective tax rate of 5%,
and the UK's proposed patent box regime, which will apply 10%
corporation tax on income from patents from April 2013.

6. Prepare for the pitfalls of intrapreneurship

In your entrepreneurial and intrapreneurial efforts, expect that the number of new products or services that actually make it to market is a fraction of the ideas that are discarded or fail market tests.

Intrapreneurs need to be given the space in which to fail, since failure is an unavoidable aspect of the intrapreneurial process. This is not to say that companies should encourage or expect failure, but rather that companies need to measure and attribute failure to either intrapreneur fault, or circumstances beyond the intrapreneur's control — and reward or reprimand accordingly.

Failure is not always the fault of the product or service. It can also have to do with timing. One of the biggest risks that an intrapreneur takes is that the market may not be ready. A prototype of the ATM, for example, was invented in 1939. After six months of field-testing, the bank discontinued its use because of low demand. It wasn't until the 1980s that ATMs made their way into mainstream banking.

Another risk issue is that of reward. Small bonuses and scarce recognition drive potential intrapreneurs away from the company to start their own businesses. While companies cannot completely prevent this brain drain, it's worth revisiting the suggestions of the original intrapreneurship experts, Gifford and Elizabeth Pinchot, who extensively researched compensation. They advocated an equitable division of profits between the intrapreneur and the employer. The Pinchots proposed that a company establish "a trusted committee to 'buy' completed research from its intrapreneurs for some pre-established fraction of its value to the company as determined by an established accounting system." Furthermore, they said, the intrapreneur "could earn in addition to his cash bonus, complete control of a definite amount of R&D funds, funds which he would have a completely free hand in investing on behalf of the corporation in his future R&D projects." By building up this "intra-capital," the innovator would have a stake in and therefore loyalty to the company.

Ultimately, personality characteristics may be the determining factor in who stays and who leaves. Intrapreneurs are almost always nonconformists. The noted leadership consultant Ken Blanchard points to other negative attributes of intrapreneurs, including insufficient transparency, lack of humility, the tendency to over-promise and under-deliver, and ignoring or rejecting checks and balances. Intrapreneurs may prefer to go it alone. A new comparative study of intrapreneurship across 11 low- and high-income countries, based on data from Babson College's Global Entrepreneurship Monitor, shows that intrapreneurship usually leads to entrepreneurship. "The incidence of nascent entrepreneurship as well as of intended entrepreneurship is higher for intrapreneurs than for other employees," note the researchers. The key takeaway from that is to realize that despite the best efforts of the company, their top intrapreneurs may leave and take their skills and dreams with them.

7. Final Thoughts

Maintenance is usually the most difficult part of any program, whether it's an individual exercise regimen or a large corporate initiative. The six strategies outlined in this chapter are most likely to succeed if implemented within an organizational framework that views intrapreneurship as an ongoing process. That means supporting it with staff, resources and formal development procedures, from the very beginnings of the idea right through to the market debut of the product or service, and the performance measurement activities. To do that, however, companies of all sizes need to set in motion behavioral changes that may challenge their conventional organizational thinking.

Create a culture of flexibility

Established companies with well-defined processes may never be as nimble as entrepreneurial startups. But they can still streamline or eliminate procedures that may prevent them from bringing an idea to market quickly. More important, though, is an organizational mindset that takes market uncertainty for granted, and develops the flexibility and resilience to deal with it in constructive ways.

At lithium-ion battery manufacturer Boston-Power, Founder and CEO Christina Lampe-Önnerud says she deliberately fosters a culture that promotes experimentation and calculated risk. "It's okay to make mistakes, just as long as you make them before you enter the market," says the scientist and Ernst & Young Entrepreneur of the Year award winner. "We do a lot of peer review and collaboration among multidisciplinary teams. But you need to give people a voice, and culture is the key to that. In other words, when processes are too strict, it's easy to say no instead of trying something new. That shuts down the entrepreneurial spirit. We're almost six years old and we still have it."

Examine your risk parameters

An intrapreneurial culture inevitably generates greater legal and financial risks for the company. In fact, in their original work on intrapreneurship, Gifford and Elizabeth Pinchot wrote that an intrapreneur should be financially prepared to take on the risks of failure, including "financial sacrifices such as having no salary increases until the new business becomes a success, or even a salary decrease until project bonuses arrive." While this may not always be feasible, companies should certainly reevaluate their risk profiles to allow for intrapreneurial efforts.

Manage internal tensions

It's not enough for intrapreneurial individuals or teams to get support from the top. Buy-in from employees of all ranks is necessary as well. Research shows that many promising ideas have been derailed by co-workers who are jealous of the attention paid to their innovative colleagues or line managers who don't want to carry a risky venture on their budgets. It's therefore vital for senior leaders to "sell" the idea of internal innovation as a tool vital for market leadership — and even survival — not only to their bosses but to everyone in the company.

Look to the long term

It's difficult to think 10 years into the future when competition is fierce today. Innovation typically requires a pipeline that takes years to develop. While incremental innovation can occur in the near term, radical innovations may require years to cultivate.

Chapter 17. Next Steps

Let the future tell the truth,
and evaluate each one according to his work and accomplishments.
The present is theirs;
the future, for which I have really worked, is mine.
Nikola Tesla
Prolific inventor and father of the modern electronics industry

With this journey now complete, you are ready to use the Opportunity Analysis Canvas to identify and analyze entrepreneurial ideas.

The Opportunity Analysis Canvas

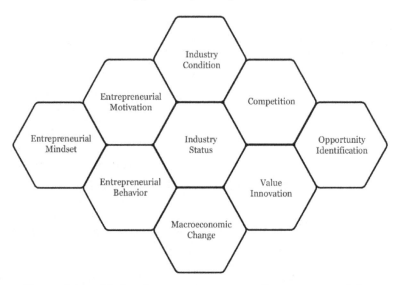

By studying this book, your awareness of entrepreneurial mindset, motivation, and behavior has expanded. You appreciate the roles of markets and industries in entrepreneurial opportunities. You understand value innovation and the fundamentals of opportunity identification as key elements of entrepreneurial action.

Developing Your Opportunity Analysis Canvas

As you develop your Opportunity Analysis Canvas, reflect on your work from prior questions in this book, and update your responses to align with this checklist.

1. Based on your prior thoughts on Thinking Entrepreneurially, summarize your level of need for achievement, individualism, control, focus, and optimism.
2. Based on your prior thoughts on Seeing Entrepreneurially, summarize your level of self-efficacy, cognitive motivation, and tolerance for ambiguity.
3. Based on your prior thoughts on Acting Entrepreneurially, summarize your confidence, risk tolerance, interpersonal relationship skills, and social capital.
4. What are the knowledge and demand conditions for a new business idea that you may develop.
    a. Include at least three references that support the demand conditions.
5. For this business idea, what is the life cycle stage of your industry, and the existing industry structure?
    a. Include at least three references that support the lifecycle stage and industry structure.
6. For this business idea, what are the demographic, psychographic, technical, and societal changes as well as the political and regulatory forces in your industry?
    a. Include at least three references that support these changes and forces.
7. For this business idea, what factors you can your team eliminate, reduce, raise, and create.

a. Describe why the factors that you all selected for the value curve are important to customers.

b. Include at least three references that support the factors that you've selected.

8. For this new business idea, discuss how the learning curve influences your success, the complementary assets that are critical to develop for your venture, and the reputation of your competitors.

    a. Include at least three references that support your analysis.

9. For this new business idea, summarize why the problem is real, how your team's solution creates value for stakeholders, the types of advantage that you all possess, and your ability to build the right team.

    a. Include at least three references that support your analysis.

Developing the Business Model

Developing your business model is the next step in your entrepreneurial journey.

As a precursor to writing the business plan, the business model describes the logic of how an organization creates, delivers, and captures value sustainably.

While the term *business model* is very popular today, the concept dates to the earliest days of business, and simply defines how an organization will make money.

A comprehensive model defines how the products or services of a business serve customer needs, at what price, through what manufacturing and distribution channels, and at what financial benefits and costs to the business.

With a well-developed business model, you can test your assumptions and strategy with prospective customers. They may affirm parts of the business model, and reject other parts. This early customer discovery and validation is valuable to adapting the business model, and perhaps the fundamental product or service idea itself, before authoring a full business plan.

Writing the Business Plan

This experience of hearing your customers' needs and wants in reaction to the business model allows you to write a well-researched business plan. With a customer-validated business plan, you can raise financial capital (if needed) and proceed with launching the venture.

Now, get to work!

Best wishes in fulfilling your entrepreneurial goals.

An idea that is developed and put into action is more important than an idea that exists only as an idea.

Edward de Bono
Physician, author, and inventor

Visit the website per the syllabus.
Enter this single-use code to
unlock your online simulation.

4633F590D6B5B08CDDAA6ED6FFFE60

CPSIA information can be obtained
at www.ICGtesting.com
Printed in the USA
LVHW012255150719
624225LV00007B/219/P